Some Same but Different
Unlearning the Concept of Disability
Second Edition

Bettina Brockmann

The proceeds of sales benefit the following scholarship for students with disabilities: Brockmann Scholarship for Students with Disabilities, SJSU Tower Foundation, account #095-4300-5194, Attn: Advancement Services 0184.

This title is available in an electronic format.

Cover image © provided by Bernd Mikus

Kendall Hunt
publishing company

www.kendallhunt.com
Send all inquiries to:
4050 Westmark Drive
Dubuque, IA 52004-1840

Copyright © 2012, 2013 by Bettina Brockmann

ISBN 978-1-4652-2680-8

Kendall Hunt Publishing Company has the exclusive rights to reproduce this work, to prepare derivative works from this work, to publicly distribute this work, to publicly perform this work and to publicly display this work.

All rights reserved. No part of this publication may be reproduced, stored in a retrieval system, or transmitted, in any form or by any means, electronic, mechanical, photocopying, recording, or otherwise, without the prior written permission of the copyright owner.

Printed in the United States of America
10 9 8 7 6 5 4 3 2 1

Contents

Some Thank You from the Editor vii
Some Foreword(s) by Dr. Deanna L. Fassett ix
Some Preface xi

CHAPTER 1: *Some Introduction* 1

Some background 1
Some voices 2
Some info about the title 3
Some info about "some" 4
Some audience 4
Some purpose 5
Some conflict 5
Some images 6
Some info about the cover 6

CHAPTER 2: *Some Motivation! Or, What's in It for Me?* 9

Some reason 9
Some conflict in motivation 11

CHAPTER 3: *Some Social Constructs* 15

Some ability, *some* disability—What do these words mean? 16
Some poetry. Or, it's just a part of who I am! 21

CHAPTER 4: *Some Understanding of Disability* 25

Some unlearning 26

Accommodation services 26
Other challenges.. 29
Some more unlearning.. 31
Notes to our professors 32

CHAPTER 5: *Some Tips on How Students and Instructors Can Create an Inclusive Environment Together* 35

Some tips for instructors... 36
The syllabus 36
Lesson plans and expectations 37
Accessibility of class material... 38
Lectures and presentation software 38
Tips to communicate with students who are deaf or
  hard of hearing 39
Communication in the classroom and beyond............................. 40
Some tips for students 41
Some wishlist... 43

CHAPTER 6: *Some Different Perspectives* 47

Some starting the conversation 49

CHAPTER 7: *Some Life Beyond Academia.* 53

Some transition... 53
Some benefits of including disability into company practices
  (working *with*) 55
Some people 55
Some planet (the work environment) 56
Some profit 57
Some tips for people with disabilities trying to enter the job market... 58

CHAPTER 8: *Some Closure* 63

APPENDIX:

Appendix A: *Some* Coauthors.. 67
    Andrew 67
    Chris 68
    Gia 69
    Jesse 70
    LuLu 71
    Vashti 71
    Yadira 73
    Bettina 74
Appendix B: DRC Accommodation Form 77
Appendix C: Unlearning Exercise 79
Appendix D: *Some* More Reading 81

Some References 83

Some Thank You From the Editor

This book was possible in large part because of team effort and students, friends, and colleagues' strong beliefs in its purpose. While some people told me to abandon the project for several reasons, others encouraged me to march on and not to turn around while halfway there. The book would not be complete without mentioning the following names and without shouting out a big "Thank You."

The biggest thank you goes out to the coauthors of this book: Andrew, Gia, Jesse, LuLu, Vashti, Yadira, and Zenon. Without you, there would not be this book. You took time out of your busy student lives to voluntarily help me with this project even though I could not promise you any compensation, just my pledge to finish this book. This became our project. You are all fun, intelligent, engaging, considerate, and committed people, and my hope is that we will continue our collaborative work for all future editions. My hope that we would continue our collaborative work for future editions has already been partly fulfilled when some of you readily agreed to work on this second edition. If you had just fallen off the radar, I might have not carried on. In addition to some anonymous contributors, our new coauthor Chris added unique insights to this edition. Thank you, Chris!

Thank you, Dr. Deanna L. Fassett, for spending hours with me on the phone providing feedback on the book while sitting in a hotel room in Detroit promoting your own book. Without your guidance as my graduate advisor and your expertise in Disability Studies and Critical Communication Pedagogy, this book would not have the insights it now exhibits.

Dana Morella-Pozzi, thank you for pushing me to not only talk to potential publishers for the book at a convention, which actually resulted in the connection with Kendall Hunt, but also for always reminding me to finish this project and for providing your critical perspectives for the draft version.

And Jeannie Kastelic, what would I do without you? I know I can always rely on you for your editing skills and your honest opinion. Your constructive feedback and thought-provoking questions made not only the first, but also this edition, so much stronger. Without your help, there might not have been a second edition—at least not now. You are definitely a coauthor! Thank you for your hard work!

Minna Holopainen, thank you for being a great friend and for telling me to not give up when others told me I should. Your advice in regard to structural editing made this book even more accessible.

Bernd Mikus, my cousin and graphic designer, thank you for patiently listening to all of our ideas and professionally converting them into this beautiful book cover.

Melissa Lamson, you might not know how your simple statement of "just do it" made me sit down and continue with this project. Also, stating that I just have to accept the fact that I cannot have everyone agreeing with my editorial choices helped a lot.

Another thank you goes out to my graduate committee members: Drs. Anne Marie Todd and Shawn Spano. Your professional feedback and support challenged me to travel outside my comfort zone and with it experiencing exciting opportunities.

Joe Wells from Kendall Hunt, thank you for believing in this book after only reading one of my emails describing this valuable project. Thank you for your patience and understanding.

Thank you, Thalia Cutsforth and Traci Vaske, Kendall Hunt's project coordinators, for your guidance, explanations, and also your patience.

My deepest appreciation goes out to the San José State University (SJSU) Disability Resource Center, especially Keri Simmons, Cindy Marota, and Maria Smyrniotis, for your continuous support and for providing useful information and forms. Without your efforts helping me to recruit students, there would not be this book.

Thank you SJSU's forensics team for letting me skip practice when the deadline of the book was just around the corner. I especially owe a lot to you, Genelle Austin-Lett and Tina Lim, as you continued supporting me even after I left forensics.

And, last but not least, my husband Markus Brockmann, my buddy, thank you for making me laugh at times when I needed it most, for believing in this project, and for providing different perspectives, of which some actually made it into this book as well.

—Bettina Brockmann

Some Foreword(s) by Dr. Deanna L. Fassett

The book you are about to read is one of a kind; I can think of no other like it. Applicable across a broad array of courses and disciplines, *Some Same but Different* invites exploration of ability and disability, both visible and nonvisible, from a critical cultural perspective. By "critical," I mean that the creators of this text have reflected on their own experiences with (dis)ability in both hopeful and challenging ways, and they invite us to do the same. In a world where we tend to ignore or stereotype disabilities, this work challenges us to consider meaningful particularities and subtleties. In an academic world that continues to breed suspicion and mistrust of disabilities in general and nonvisible disabilities (like certain learning disabilities or psychiatric disorders) in particular, this work challenges us to open our minds and find common ground.

What marks *Some Same but Different* as truly unique, however, is Brockmann's approach as researcher and editor of this work. Embracing a critical approach, one that is attentive to power and culture as constituted or created in communication, Brockmann worked with and elicited input from students who have a wide variety of (dis)abilities. Rather than writing *to* students with disabilities or writing *for* students with disabilities—in either case assuming a position of knowledge and superiority that might silence her colleagues—Brockmann worked toward praxis: reflection and action (of *all* participants in this project) on the world in order to transform it. This work helps bring us all one step closer to better understanding how to engage one another in dialogue across difference. Further, it brings us all one step closer to better understanding the role of communication in creating and challenging prejudice and misunderstanding.

As you work through this book, I hope you'll take seriously the invitation to explore your own understandings and assumptions regarding (dis)ability, but I also hope you'll consider what sort of work you might undertake in this vein yourself. How might you become an advocate (*with* others, not *for* others) regarding issues, questions, and problems that are meaningful to you and the people you love? Please also know that, as a work in evolution, your thoughts about this book will also help to strengthen and breathe life into it for many years to come. That your own insights and experiences can play a role in revising a work that gives back to and strengthens us all is an exciting proposition.

I, for one, am very eager to see how this work continues to evolve; from conception to execution, *Some Same but Different* has been novel, meaningful, and exciting. It begins to fill an important and vast chasm in (dis)ability-related research and pedagogy in communication studies, and it is a model from which we might all learn and grow, whether as individuals, as students, or as educators. In what directions will you take the lessons you learn here?

Deanna L. Fassett, Ph.D.
Professor, Department of Communication Studies
San José State University
27 August 2011

Some Preface

Welcome to the dynamic process that is: this book. A lot of exciting themes exhibited in this book developed through collaborative and explorative work. This book is full of ambiguity and ambivalence, and I feel this is what makes it so special. Whatever you are looking for, you won't find *the* answer here but rather an invitation to engage in the—maybe for some uncomfortable—process of exploring one's own inner attitudes toward (dis)ability. Do not make this a fast read but rather stop after each section for a few minutes to reflect, to consider your own role and position in society's hierarchical system.

In this short preface, I want to share some developments that highlight why and how this book can be a strong transformative tool. At *some* point, you can imagine where I am heading now, the mundane word *some* started appearing within this book in somehow meaningful ways. I played with its ambivalence and its difference in meaning depending on context and emphasis, such as "here is some information" (indifferent) in contrast to "wow, this is *some* information!" (compelling). In addition, I appreciate how *some* suggests potential and opportunity for growth. As a result, the word *some* became an essential part of this book as it represents and relates to the concept of disability. The concept of disability, often surrounded by negative attitudes and beliefs, and its potential to impact our society positively is often underestimated. This book will bring to light the often hidden and unrecognized opportunities disability represents.

This brings me to my question: What do *you* think is "the concept of disability"? Do you associate it with something positive or negative, exciting or boring? As you can imagine reading the subtitle, we assume that the overall concept is at a state that needs to be transformed. By associating the word *disability* with expressions such as enjoy and exciting, we already start the unlearning process. Unlearning—another concept that suddenly showed up at our meetings without invitation. However, we also saw its potential and decided for it to become part of this book as well. I will not unpack the concept of unlearning here in the preface—what would then be the purpose of reading this book? We want you, the reader, to find out for yourself. Do *you* think there is a difference between learning and unlearning? If so, what is it?

I am excited, nervous, and eager to see how *you* make meaning of this book's concepts and how *you* interpret and feel about them. I would love to hear if and how it transformed and affected you on a personal and/or professional level. In addition to providing your input, my hope is that this book inspires you to partake in similar projects.

Now, I invite you to enjoy and engage in the compelling world of disability.
—Bettina Brockmann

Chapter 1

Some Introduction

SOME BACKGROUND

Listening to and interacting with others who are different from us is an opportunity for personal growth and enlightenment. In Bettina's experience of working with students with disabilities, she came to know her own ignorant self and learned from the students how to be a better person.

During her work in the skills center at a community college, Bettina had two experiences that resulted in a sudden revelation of her own participation in the construct of disability. The first one occurred after a student using a wheelchair came into the center dripping wet. Though Bettina had worked in the center for several years, up to that point she had not been aware that the center did not have an automatic door opener. She had not been aware that students using wheelchairs had to wait outside, sometimes in the pouring rain, until someone would open the door for them. These realizations inspired Bettina to collaborate with one of the students to begin a letter-writing campaign that would enable the center to obtain the door opener. Fortunately, after two long years, they were finally successful and celebrated with a ribbon-cutting ceremony.

The second epiphany happened after Bettina talked with a student who had been diagnosed with both bipolar and schizophrenia. During the conversation, they realized that they actually lived close to each other. Surprisingly, though, on her way home that night, Bettina was suddenly overcome by fear when she thought of him living in her neighborhood. Bettina, shocked by her reaction, became inspired to investigate the source of her unfounded concern. After some soul searching, she understood that her lack of knowledge about this student's diagnoses was to blame for her irrational feelings. Because mental illness is highly stigmatized in today's society, people often avoid confronting this uncomfortable topic resulting in this type of ignorance.

These two experiences inspired Bettina to focus her work on disability, and she is excited not only to be involved in meaningful work, but also to have learned from the students how to not be afraid to confront her own ignorance. They encouraged her to explore means to help other people experience similar revelations about their own ignorance toward topics they might avoid because of uncertainty and stigmatization. This book is one of those means.

The collaboration that led to the creation of this book started as a graduate project. The courses Bettina took as a Communication Studies major touched on a number of diversity issues, but she quickly discovered that discussions about disability and ableism[1] fell short. Her goal became to change that by creating a book that would open up diversity conversations to disabilities. However, Bettina was also aware that she, as a person who is not considered disabled, could not have sincerely and honestly discussed or written about a topic she had not experienced firsthand. Therefore, Bettina invited students living with disabilities to write the book about their experiences.

This book offers a model for praxis-oriented communication, how to work *with* (not *for* or *on*) people with disabilities. Writing and working *with* helps to create inclusion and, as this book shows, results in solution-oriented and effective teamwork! The team met regularly throughout a semester, and our discussions and conversations are what you will see in this book. For this second edition, the team met several times to discuss what has changed since the first edition was published and what experiences should be added to the book. We lost a few voices and gained a few, and these dynamic changes became part of the revisions.

SOME VOICES

At this point, you might be wondering why the person who is stated as the author on the book's cover writes in the third person. This decision developed as part of the editing process when investigating ways on how to share the students' (from now on referred to as coauthors) insights in a compelling and readable manner. After long consideration, Bettina, the editor, decided to refer to herself as "Bettina" instead of "I" to not differentiate herself too much from the coauthors.

---

1 The discrimination against people with disabilities. Automatic spell checkers often still underline ableism as a misspelled word; this indicates that it is still not as commonly known as other "isms."

Initially, Bettina wanted the entire book to only consist of the coauthors' voices; her only task would have been that of an editor. However, she realized that she too had become part of this conversation, and it would be misleading to take her voice completely out of this book. Moreover, as a facilitator, she might have, unknowingly, guided the discussions in a specific direction. So, Bettina became part of the collective and used "we" or "us" to incorporate all the voices cohesively even though not every participant might have experienced the events described directly.

Some of us coauthors did not want to identify ourselves and so used pseudonyms for the introductions in the "Some Coauthors" appendix. To not jeopardize the anonymity of those with pseudonyms, we did not assign names to individual comments—as they could reveal identifying characteristics—but just refer to "one of the coauthors" (except for the "*Some* Poetry" and "*Some Different Perspectives*" sections). Plus, we did not want to make it appear as if some coauthors contributed more to the conversation than others in the event that some names would appear more often. For the second edition, we were still working from a first-edition core group. As mentioned before, we lost a few authors but gained others.

The hesitancy of using real names on a project like this demonstrates how unsafe some of us feel within the educational system today. We worry about repercussions by instructors. Others, especially those of us with non-visible disabilities (i.e., disabilities that are not immediately perceived by others), are aware of the stigma associated with disability and are afraid to reveal ourselves and our disabilities in front of classmates. In the context of disability, we define stigma as negative stereotypical characteristics that an ableist society ascribes to people with disabilities. We do not want to share these stereotypes since this would only participate in their perpetuation. With this book, you will learn to adopt a more positive attitude toward the word *disability*.

SOME INFO ABOUT THE TITLE

Some Same but Different is, at least in our opinion, a clever adaptation of the saying "same same but different." The meaning of "same same but different" depends on the context and the interpretation of the user. So this leaves us some leeway on how to make sense of our book. *Some Same but Different* relates to our team of coauthors since we are a fun and diverse group of college students. The fact that we are associated with our university's disability center brought us together, but there are so many other things we have in common and so many things that differentiate us. We have in common our dedication to education, our struggles as students with disabilities, and our strong beliefs in our abilities and potentials. But we are different in gender, culture, race, religious outlooks, economic status, family status, and so on, and we also differ in our disabilities and in our abilities.

We all care for each other and the other students on campus; we love to learn, and we are very ambitious. We have to be since our path to succeed as students with disabilities in the traditional academic environment is paved with many obstacles. Regardless, our attitude toward being different remains positive. We believe different is cool since it produces a variety of opinions, attitudes, and perspectives, and this is what makes our lives so rich.

SOME INFO ABOUT *"SOME"*

This is a book in progress, and our hope is to expand it with the help of you, the reader. As with any other diversity issue, the topic of disability is too complex to even pretend that this could be a comprehensive guide, but it should serve as a conversation starter. This book will not have all the answers you look for regarding issues surrounding disability, but it will provide *some*. Therefore, in addition to the title, the chapter titles also include the expression *some*, and with your help, this *some* will develop into more.

The release of the book has inspired meaningful discussions that led to this enhanced second version. The book has been incorporated in Argumentation and Advocacy, Intercultural Communication, and Professional Business Communication courses. Bettina took the book to her native country Germany and presented and taught about inclusion and accessibility at German universities—topics that just recently became of interest to German schools due to the ratification of the UN Convention on the Rights of Persons with Disabilities.[2] All of these conversations and experiences have evolved the some in *some*.

SOME AUDIENCE

When starting this project, we planned on addressing the entire academic audience including students, faculty, and staff. Our intention is still to reach all these groups, but we are also aware that, as a textbook, the majority of readers will be students. Therefore, as another editorial choice, the "you" in this book

2   http://www.un.org/disabilities/convention/conventionfull.shtml

presumes the readership of students in higher education as the primary audience—and instructors, and now also employers, as the secondary audience. Because some of us have left academia since the first edition, we decided to add an additional chapter focusing on life beyond academia. The "*Some* Life beyond Academia" section focuses on employers as the main audience. Employers need to understand what experiences their employees with disabilities had in higher education. This understanding will participate in the creation of a more effective and collaborative diversity management. We encourage employers to read all chapters as this is important in setting the context, and discussions in the earlier chapters also apply to business life.

However, we do not want to stop the conversation by limiting the scope of our audience, so we invite everyone to engage in the dialogic interaction.

SOME PURPOSE

Therefore, the purpose is to have a wider audience contributing to our conversations surrounding ability and disability. We encourage other people with disabilities to share their own personal experiences with their specific disabilities in educational and non-educational settings to help broaden our understanding even further. This continued sharing also serves as a way to be and stay connected and show the world that even though you have a disability, you are not alone. The email option noted below can serve as an outlet for both students and instructors, and is also an invitation to continue the conversation beyond the limits of this book. Please email your comments and suggestions to *somesamebutdifferent@gmail.com*, and we will continue making an effort to include them in one of our next editions. As a book in progress, this conversation will grow with our readers' contributions, and this second edition already demonstrates how meaningful input adds substance to the discussion.

SOME CONFLICT

"But it is the struggle that represents hope; it is only in and through that discomfort that we learn to listen and seek community, seek possibility" (Fassett & Warren, 2007, p. 88).

The goal of this book is not necessarily to create harmony and avoid conflict. Actually, the thought-provoking, and at times intense, discussions inspired by presentations of this book at conferences and in classes generated our desire to revise the first edition. Therefore, we feel that conflict can be the means to bring about change; staying oblivious and not acknowledging and exploring one's own inner beliefs and feelings, even if they might be scary and frightening, will lead to superficial and, at times, ignorant behavior. Rather, we want you to feel the tension; we want you to struggle with your ingrained stereotypes about people with disabilities. We invite you to engage in this struggle, this tension; be curious, and give yourself permission to change forever by learning more about you and your relationships with others. This is the real benefit of this book!

SOME IMAGES

For this second edition we now also have the honor to exhibit some of Jesse's drawings. Jesse is a talented artist who creates unique and original pieces. Jesse shares that his artwork is "inspired by my imagination with the intent for others to interpret with their own imaginations." We invite you to explore his work by taking the time to immerse yourself in the images and to create your own meaning. To enhance this experience, interpret the artwork first before taking a look at Jesse's interpretation. Please also check out Jesse's blog to admire his work in color: http://jessenatchezmolina.blogspot.com.

SOME INFO ABOUT THE COVER

During one of our discussions about the cover design, one coauthor shared with us that she had a dream about a possible cover for our book, and she explained how and why this cover would relate to our project:

> *When I talk to myself in the mirror, I'm true to myself. I need reassurance somehow besides my prayers. I tell myself, you can do it. Don't get scared. No matter how hard this material is going to be, you can do it. Don't give up. If you see yourself in the mirror, you know your limitations. We all know our limitations as individuals. But inside of you, you have to get strength from somewhere to tell yourself, no matter what your limitations are, you can do this. I see I have more ability than disability, and I have to, all of us, have to work harder. We have to work so much harder just to get at the same level as the rest of the class.*

We all liked her imagery and her explanation, so now her dream has been realized on the front cover.

What would you see in the mirror?

Some Introduction 7

Name _____ **Date** _____

Think about it:

1. What does the word *disability* evoke in you? Without evaluation or contemplation, quickly write down the thoughts and feelings you associate with this word.

Keep this list for now. We will come back to it at the end of the book.

After providing some of the background in the development of this book, we will now start exploring why there actually is a need for a book like this. Let's begin by looking at the big picture: society, language, the social constructs of disability, and what we can do to really invite and include diversity issues such as disability into the educational arena.

2. How do you feel about Bettina's decision of writing in third-person voice? How would you have handled the situation?

3. How do you feel about people writing or talking about a group of which they are not considered a member? Or about people who talk about topics they are not directly affected by or have no personal experience with (e.g., men discussing abortion/pro life, people evaluating cultural rituals or behaviors of foreign cultures, white professors teaching black history)? In your discussions, consider addressing topics such as generalization, stereotypes, and ethnocentrism. Support your arguments with examples. What strategies do you feel would achieve justified and righteous representation?

4. (connect to Think about it 3 to set context) In her book *Teaching to Transgress: Education as the Practice of Freedom*, bell hooks (1994) discusses the "privileged standpoint," the "unique mixture of experiential and analytical ways of knowing. ... It cannot be acquired through books or even distanced observation and study of a particular reality.... This privileged standpoint does not emerge from the 'authority of experience' but rather from the passion of experience, the passion of remembrance" (p. 90). What do you think hooks means by this "privileged position"? Do you agree with her statement? Why? Why not?

chapter 2

Some Motivation! Or, What's in It for Me?

SOME REASON

In today's capitalist and consumer-driven world, everything is about profits and personal benefits. In this fast-paced environment, the questions "What's in it for me?" and "Is it worth spending my valuable time?" are always at the back of our minds. Diversity coaches nowadays attempt to inspire managers to be interested in diversity workshops by asserting that well-managed multicultural teams are much more effective than mono-cultural teams—the emphasis is on "well-managed." Efficient collaboration and valuing and incorporating different viewpoints have long been the success strategy for many companies. And this is true for disability as well.

Another motivation for companies should be today's significant information on demographics, which now demand greater inclusion of the diverse groups within society. With an estimated population of 650 million, people living with disabilities are the largest minority group in the world (United Nations, 2006). And with an estimated population of 54 million, people with disabilities also comprise the largest minority group in the United States (U.S. Census Bureau, 2008, p. 3). For businesses, not incorporating disability and accessibility into business strategies would mean missing out on a large number of potential customers and the opportunity to hire valuable and creative employees who can relate to a more extensive market. We will discuss this in more detail in the "*Some* Life beyond Academia" chapter.

Already many of us benefit from the insights and contributions of people with disabilities every day. For example, universal access technology, technology designed to facilitate computer use for people with disabilities, eases the computer use for most of us, thus the term "universal." Screen magnifiers, adaptive keyboards, voice over, etc., make life easier for many of us. Some people use voice over, also referred to as text-to-speech function, when they are tired of reading. This function has been designed for people who are blind or dyslexic, and it is also extremely useful for most of us. On a Mac, you can adjust these settings under System Preferences and Universal Access. On a PC, you can find similar options with the Control Panel. Probably most of us have used the zoom tool to enlarge difficult to read items on our screens. We owe all of these helpful adjustments to people with disabilities.

Besides universal access technology, "Universal Design" refers to general design adjustments that work well for everyone. To illustrate, curb cuts, the ramps from sidewalk to street level, were initially installed to aide people with disabilities, but they also benefit bike riders, parents with strollers, delivery people, and others as well.

Of course, in addition to learning about technology and other universal designs, we also personally benefit in other ways from interacting with people with disabilities. For example, one day, after having attended an informative presentation by an Internet corporation's accessibility lab on our campus, Bettina sat down on a bench next to one of the presenters while they waited for his ride back. This speaker, who had lost his eyesight as a child, said to her: "This is a beautiful campus. Are there lots of students sitting outside studying?" Surprised by his statement, and his subsequent questions, Bettina started looking around. She described the campus to him, and in doing so, felt like she really saw it for the first time. It is a beautiful campus, she thought, admiring the palm trees lining the plaza and experiencing the dynamic atmosphere that college campuses emanate. She realized that if he had not asked, she might have never realized how lucky she was to study at such a lovely university.

So you see, there is a lot in it for you! We are sure that reading this book will provide you with similar positive insights. When students and instructors work together, everyone benefits. In fact, studies relating to Universal Design for Learning (a similar concept as universal access and universal design but applied to the educational system) show that curricula and lesson plan adjustment to accommodate students with disabilities benefitted all students (Zeff, 2007). Often instructors worry that these adaptations would decrease the value of the course and would make it too easy to pass. We agree that school should be rigorous to prepare students for other challenges ahead, but the goal is not to create an effortless environment; the goal is to create an unbiased and fair environment where everyone can work to her/his own fullest potential. Creating this environment requires opening our minds to invite different perspectives. So, go ahead, open your mind, and you will see that we can all benefit from each other.

SOME CONFLICT IN MOTIVATION

The creation of some parts of this chapter involved conflict and uneasiness as we employed reasoning informed by dominant societal standards. While we do not want to support and encourage a materialistic mindset and lifestyle, we still have to accept that we are part of the system. Numbers and monetary compensation might, unfortunately, be the main means by which we make our voices heard in a capitalist world. Nonetheless, our discussion should not devalue the environment we envision; an environment in which we define ourselves not by *what* we have but by *how* we respectfully interact with others. We believe that sustainability and accessibility go hand in hand, and that sensible and reasonable communication can transgress to a state where these concepts guide our societal practices.

Some Motivation! Or, What's in It for Me? 13

Name _____ **Date** _____

Think about it:

Have you ever had someone make you see some of life's beauties you took for granted?

Action Items:

1. Walk around your campus or neighborhood and really open your eyes. Make a list of things you have never recognized before. Compare and discuss your list with classmates.

2. Watch the movie *The Intouchables*.

   To provide some background: The story of this movie is based on the life of Philippe Pozzo di Borgo who became quadriplegic after a paragliding accident and the relationship with his caretaker Driss. In real life, Philippe often comments that he doesn't want pity as he finds pity hopeless.

   While watching the movie, take notes about how you feel the main protagonists Philippe and Driss benefit from and motivate each other. Discuss with classmates.

3. Read the "Some facts about persons with disabilities" on the United Nations Convention on the Rights of Persons with Disabilities website: http://www.un.org/disabilities/convention/facts.shtml. Which of these facts do you find most surprising? Why do you think the UN includes these facts on the website? What do you feel is their motivation?

4. Do some research on the terms *sustainability*, *accessibility*, and *inclusion*. Write down a definition for each and look for similarities of these concepts. Can you envision an environment that combines all three concepts? What would this world look like and what could we do to achieve this?

chapter 3

Some Social Constructs...

"Communication does more than represent social reality, it actually creates it!" (Spano, 2010, p. 4).

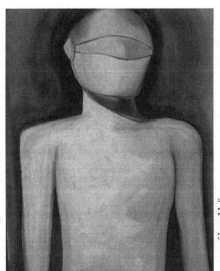

Title: GORT, Medium: Oil on Canvas, Year: 2012, Original in Color

Courtesy of Jesse Molina

Many people approach disability from a medical rather than from a social perspective where the "cure" of disabilities lies in medicating the symptoms and in inspiring people with disabilities to find means to "overcome" their disabilities. In this context, "overcoming" refers to emulating this society's ideal of the "normal and able" body. The idea of this standard is constituted in language and culture; thus, disability is socially constructed by dominant cultural practices. We all participate in this process, often unconsciously, by reiterating and affirming the status quo and the ideal of normalcy. With our discussions, we want to challenge current understandings of what constitutes "the norm" and to illuminate the cultural practices that give rise to the social construct of disability. Our awareness of these confining practices can assist us in constructing standards that do not marginalize.

A person using a wheelchair told this story: One day at a supermarket, a mother freaked out when her daughter came to touch his wheelchair. She just grabbed the little toddler's arm, screamed at her, and pulled her away. He then asked, so what do we teach kids through these types of behaviors? He went on to say that his own daughter learned a different attitude toward wheelchairs. She LOVES riding in it on her father's lap and beams with pride that her father owns such a fancy ride.

This story suggests that we *learn* how to socialize with people who are different from us. Studies show that kids at an early age approach people with disabilities with curious and honest interest, but soon they learn to avoid interaction from imitating their parents and other caregivers. We embrace the theory that the attitude toward people with disabilities is a learned behavior since this promises that people can unlearn. Contrary to learning, which is often an unconscious process, unlearning means consciously engaging in an investigation of one's own inner beliefs; unlearning means self-reflection and opening one's mind to diverse viewpoints—consequently offering the possibility for social change. With this in mind, this book serves as a catalyst to help you, the reader, gain a new perspective about people with disabilities and about people who are not like you. We want to help with the unlearning process by showing you who we really are. We know that many people feel pity when seeing a person with a disability. We do not want pity—as we are not pitiful. Belittling and condescending remarks and thoughts often participate even more in our disability than the biological aspects. So though we know there are many barriers that participate in the creation of disability, such as an inaccessible building, for the purpose of this book, we are specifically going to focus on behavior and language choices.

SOME ABILITY, *SOME* DISABILITY— WHAT DO THESE WORDS MEAN?

In addition to our behavior, language plays an essential role in the social construct of disability. Everyday language participates in creating negative connotations of disability with expressions such as "that's lame," "that's retarded," "crippled economy," and "disabled train." Typically, we do not reflect on the hidden meanings of these words; we are often not aware that they imply that disability is dismissive. However, people with disabilities are aware of this implication. When discussing the term *disability* within our group, these were some of our comments:

> *I hate that term! It makes me feel like an outcast, makes me feel stupid. It places me below my classmates.*

> *Dysphemism is the opposite of euphemism. The term* disabled *has become a dysphemism because people who are not disabled place people with challenges below them.*

As a group, we learned a lot about each other and the pervasiveness of the negative connotation associated with the word *disability*, and we learned how this idea sneaks into *all* of our minds. In 2009, Bettina participated in a workshop at a veterans hospital on how community colleges could support students with mild traumatic brain injury and post traumatic stress disorder. Many of the soldiers and counselors shared how difficult it is for soldiers, whose daily-recited creed includes: "I will never accept defeat. I will never quit" (The soldier's creed, 2005), to walk into a place like a disability center that has, in huge and bold letters, the word "disabled" written over the door. Some felt that if they walked underneath those words and stepped into that center, they disrespected their warrior ethos and accepted defeat. We hope they know by now that students associated with disability centers are anything but quitters.

People with disabilities have to work extremely hard to achieve social inclusion, and their efforts are often not recognized. Bettina shared a story with us about a half-marathon she attended in Long Beach, California, that provided some context to this idea. Before the start of the race, the announcer said, "We first start with the wheelchair racers, then we listen to the National Anthem, and then we have the start of the able racers." After finishing the story, she asked: "What message did this send?" To us, this announcement, even if not intended, communicated that the wheelchair racers were not really part of the race. Probably everyone has experienced the energy and excitement a crowd produces when listening to the National Anthem, and this group of athletes was excluded from participating in this community-building event. Plus, by saying "able" racers, the announcer implied that the wheelchair racers were *not* able. These are often world-class athletes, and they were not acknowledged the same way as all the other racers. (FYI, Bettina contacted the organizers of the marathon, and they apologized, promising to change this type of communication in the future.) The subtleness of such defining messages often evades our awareness, resulting in a continuous dissemination of the idea to best avoid being associated with terms like disabled. We wonder if society could come up with a different expression, would this in fact change how people perceive disability, or if, after a few years, the same stigma surrounding disability would attach itself to the new expression?

When discussing terms like these in communication courses and how they create meaning, students usually say that these discussions are just hypersensitive. They comment that they do not mean it that way and that it is just fun, and we should not overanalyze things. You might remember when President Barack Obama on the *Tonight Show* with Jay Leno compared his bad bowling skills to Special Olympics and the following outrage that occurred. Jay Leno should have responded: "Wow, you're that good???" See how easily it happens. Apparently, President Obama apologized to the Special Olympics Committee even before the show aired (Tapper, 2009). We understand that these terms and expressions are part of our everyday language, and that we often do not mean to offend others. We do not want people to always feel guilty, but instead we want to assist people with developing an increased awareness of discourse's, often subtle, implications.

These words represent us. Some of us are rather confident and do not mind at all being considered disabled first. The Deaf community purposely capitalizes Deaf as a signal that deafness defines them. And maybe also to defy society's standards of what is considered normal. Freire (1992) states that "changing language is part of the process of changing the world" (p. 68). So, until society has a more positive attitude toward disability, we suggest a few language choices that could help with the process of creating a more inclusive environment:
- Saying "person with a disability" instead of "disabled person" helps to see the person first, and not the disability.
- Saying "non-disabled" instead of "able" communicates that being non-disabled is not necessarily the norm, the status quo. When we describe someone as able, we imply that others are *not* able.
- Saying someone uses a wheelchair instead of expressions such as "wheelchair-bound" or "confined to a wheelchair." The last two expressions often imply a negative association with the wheelchair. However, some people using a wheelchair shared with us that the wheels meant freedom to them. A person, who received donations through *San Jose Mercury News*' "make a wish" program, proudly showed us his new ride with all its features and technological advancements. Another person told us that after an active lifestyle including running, she initially felt the restrictions of the wheelchair; however, she does not associate it with the terms *confinement* or *bound* anymore. Because of the chair, she can get to the swimming pool where she can now continue her physical activities. This should not diminish some people's adjustment period to a wheelchair, but maybe a less negative communicative association would help with that process.

Still, it bothers us that society and hegemonic discourse force us to consider language changes like these. A wealthy person would not complain about being considered wealthy first. The same applies to a successful, caring, able, athletic, etc. person. Being on a Hawaiian-bound flight also does not sound too bad to us. Maybe, instead of the language adjustments, we should modify the overall meaning we associate with the previously mentioned terms, so a disabled train refers to an extremely fast train like the Intercity Express (ICE) in Germany, something that's lame is unbelievably exciting and thrilling, a crippled economy is an economy at its peak, and a disabled student is a student who excels. What do you think?

Some Social Constructs...

Name _____ **Date** _____

Think about it:

How will you teach your kids, grandkids, nieces, or nephews how to interact with people who are different from you?

Action items:

1. Watch your favorite show and make a list of words and comments that participate in the creation of a positive or negative identity of a specific group such as the elderly, immigrants, etc.

2. What do you think is the difference between learning and unlearning? Write a list of behaviors and attitudes you wish you could unlearn. Keep this list for now, we will come back to it in the next section (Appendix C).

3. Go to http://www.ted.com/talks and find a speech relating to disability, for example speeches by Sue Austin, Aimee Mullins, or Caroline Casey. How do you feel the speeches help you with unlearning the concept of disability? Or, do they also participate in the social construct of disability? Do they offer new insights by challenging your view of disability? Provide specific examples and discuss.

SOME POETRY... OR, IT'S JUST A PART OF WHO I AM!

Through these language and behavior patterns, we often label people as something they are not. Without even knowing a person, we assign characteristics based on stereotypes and societal standards. What do you think when you see a beautiful young woman with a walker? Vashti shared this poem with us in one meeting, and we all had no doubt that this belongs in the book.

When you look at me
—Vashti

When you look at me, what do you see?
Do you see a girl who is disabled?
I see a girl who loves sports.
Do you see me as dependent?
I am as independent as they come.
Do your eyes fall immediately on my walker,
Or do you notice the pep in my step?
Are you blinded by my disabled license plate,
Or by my beautiful smile?
Are you staring at the braces on my legs,
Or my great calves?
When you see tears in my eyes,
Do you think it is from pain in my heart?
Or can you see that I laugh so hard that I shed tears?
Do you see a girl struggling to get across campus?
Or do you see a girl who refuses to let her disability hold her back?
Do you see a girl who needs help?
Or do you see a girl who lives to help others?
Do you think that I don't see you when you look at me?
Look at me all you want,
But remember that when you look at me,
What you think you see is not always reality.

This poem shows that a labeling and stigmatizing gaze can contribute more to our disability than the actual physical disability itself. As mentioned earlier, our goal is to help people see the individual first and not to categorize a person by visible or other stereotypical characteristics. Of course, the idiom "Don't judge a book by its cover" also applies to other diversity issues. And, disability is just another of the many layers of diversity such as race, gender, economical status, political viewpoint, religious views, etc.—none of these solely define us; they are only part of us. It is often the environment that disables, and we all participate in the creation of disability through that environment. So this book is just the first step in helping you, the reader, to rethink, and if necessary to unlearn, the behavior you use when getting to know others.

Some Social Constructs... 23

Name _____ **Date** _____

Think about it:

What do you feel/think when you see a person with a disability?

Action item:

How do you see yourself? What do you think others see in you? Ask a few people (e.g., friends, family members, instructors, students) about how they perceive you. How does this differ/not differ from how you see yourself? How did this make you feel?

chapter 4

Some Understanding of Disability

Disability is associated with a variety of stigmas and stereotypes, and we are aware that our book somehow contributes to this as well. By sharing our experiences, we ourselves are participating in the creation of disability identities. To counteract this theme, we want to inspire and challenge you to really listen to us, to each other, without immediate categorization. Therefore, we decided *not* to include a section describing a variety of disabilities and their diagnostic characteristics in this book, since that would only contribute to the notion of defining people according to some label. Without that defining label, we instead need to get to know others first to understand their needs.

To illustrate, when Bettina was working in an academic skills center at a community college, the campus's disability center often sent students to this center for further skill-building. The conversation with the student started with an initial student-instructor conference, which allowed the instructor to learn more about the student before creating an individualized, self-paced instructional program. The center's research library was based on the "traditional" student, and the instructors of the skills center initially often wondered if their chosen assignments were actually appropriate for the student's specific disability. Therefore, they asked the disability center to offer a workshop teaching them about the learning styles and characteristics of different disabilities. The disability center kindly declined stating that the skills center program was so helpful for the students because instructors did not pick suggested exercises from any preconceived table or chart, but instead initiated a conversation with students first and then built a program together.

This learning environment highlights how conversations with us, the students, assist more with comprehending our specific needs than generic assumptions. And, we can be very creative in elucidating our challenges. At one point, Bettina attended a faculty workshop led by students with disabilities, and it offered some insights into students' daily efforts. The students asked the workshop participants to write with their non-dominant hand when taking notes while listening to a mini-lecture. Needless to say, when the lecture was over, most of the faculty could not even remember what the lecture was about; they only remembered their struggle to put something legible on their papers. This is one reason why students should be the primary resource for educators and others when trying to understand their disabilities; otherwise, the educational environment will continue ascribing general characteristics that will not lead to a beneficial and satisfying result for all parties involved.

SOME UNLEARNING

The unlearning process should be initiated by assessing the current situation. Our group's initial discussion sessions were geared toward this goal, and they seemed to serve the purpose of catharsis since we embraced the opportunity to share our experiences as students with disabilities. Without a doubt, we needed the space to vent, to realize we were not alone, and that the hurdles we faced were not unique to us individually. After these sessions, Bettina shared with us that she felt an initial sense of satisfaction that she was able to provide such a space, and she just sat back and listened. Then, the satisfaction turned into frustration, frustration with herself, her own ignorance, and how her privilege as a non-disabled person (in this context, she described herself as non-disabled first) made her not realize and not see some of the obvious obstacles students with disabilities have to face on a daily basis. Her frustration, struggle, and self-reflection actually initiated her personal unlearning process. To help you, the reader, engage in this process, we now share our experiences to add some perspective to what it really means to be a student with a disability in higher education.

Accommodation Services

The accommodation process is a bit complex, so let us provide some context. Accommodation refers to students with disabilities receiving support services such as extra time for tests, a sign language interpreter, a note-taker, etc. The specific processes and requirements differ among campuses, and students and instructors would do well to check with their disability centers. The following information is based on our university's policies. First, we have to self-identify and provide appropriate documentation at the campus's Disability Resource

Center (DRC). Every university has specific requirements and guidelines, and obtaining the documentation, including assessment tests, often comes at high costs. Some community colleges still offer free testing, but because of budget cuts, these services have been cut more and more. Then, if we qualify for services, we receive an accommodation form explaining the specific accommodation services. This form is a three-way contract between us, the instructor, and the DRC. We have to initiate the process and set up an appointment with the instructor to discuss the accommodation options. We decided to include a sample in this book to familiarize students and instructors with the specific language (Appendix B). Once the instructor has signed the form, we have to return the document to the DRC on time. From then on, we have to be very organized to ensure staying on top of a variety of required timelines for setting up the specific services. So, let's take a look at what the specific services really mean for us (i.e., assessing the current situation).

Approaching the instructor
We do not enjoy this step of the process, especially since we often feel we have to defend ourselves as some instructors express suspicion about asking for accommodation. For example, one of us with a non-visible learning disability had to respond to "Are you sure you need this (accommodation)? You don't look disabled..." A coauthor with a visible disability shared: "I have had teachers ask me what was wrong with me. Not sure if they meant it negatively, but it is uncomfortable to have to defend my disability to someone. I have had teachers flat out refuse to give me accommodations. It is like we are fighting against our teachers like we are in the wrong." Because of a variety of uncomfortable encounters like these, we learned to pick our battles and often try to get through a class without asking for accommodation, especially if an instructor appears inaccessible. Some of us feel the struggle trying to pass a course without the required services is at times more bearable than being treated as a cheater.

Extra time
Some of us receive extra time for taking a test. However, the expression "extra" is misleading as experiences with classmates and instructors show. We had classmates tell us, "You have extra time for your tests? Lucky you!" And a professor said to one of us once, "You should've done better; you had extra time." But, the extra time is not about creating an advantage over others—there are several reasons why we require the extra time—some because of a physical and some because of a learning disability. Nevertheless, we have to know the material and study hard. The extra time students with disabilities receive is geared toward

creating an equal playing field. We need the extra time because it takes us a bit longer to comprehend things. We are not really getting *extra* time because it takes us the entire time to do what other students can do within their assigned time.

And, it is not only tests and exams that take us longer to complete but every reading and homework assignment as well. We do not get extra time or extensions for that. This means that as students with disabilities, we have to work extra hard to succeed in college.

Taking the test on your own
Universities provide testing centers where the students can take exams in privacy, free of disturbance and interruptions. We find our campus's testing center to be comfortable, allowing us to focus and concentrate on the task at hand, which we could not do in a cramped classroom. However, this service still offers a few challenges, as we have to take the test on our own without the opportunity of asking the instructor for clarification—a benefit other students have:

> *Once after a test, I talked to classmates about the confusion I had about a part of the exam. They told me that the instructor explained this in class during the test after students asked for explanation. Since I wasn't there, I was the only one who missed this section. I hate that I can't ask questions during the test!*

In addition, our testing center, even though comfortable, is located in a very old and inaccessible building, resulting in additional obstacles for some of us:

> *In the beginning, they did not stop the clock when I had to use the bathroom. You have to take two doors to get to the lady's bathroom, and they are heavy! There is no automatic door opener. It is very difficult to navigate through the two doors with a walker, let alone a wheelchair. And the lady's restroom is at the other end of the hallway, the men's restroom is right there—once I used that one out of distress. With my walker, I have to walk slowly—it takes at least 10 minutes for me to get to the bathroom and back. During a longer exam, I lost about 30 minutes' exam time.*

Thus, even though we appreciate these services tremendously, the statements show the reality of receiving "special" services.

Pop-quizzes
In this context, it is also important to address the issue of pop-quizzes. Often, instructors told us that we shouldn't complain about having to take short tests

in class. The problem we have with these types of quizzes does not have to do with time but with an environment in which we can't concentrate on the topic at hand. If people are moving chairs and start leaving class hanging outside chatting, we lose focus and blank out. Also, the little noises like paper shuffling and pencil movement amplify for us. It's crucial for us to take tests in complete silence. And, of course, we feel embarrassed if everyone has to wait for us... Some of us are in a constant fear of facing situations in the traditional classroom we cannot handle. It creates a very stressful environment.

Note-taking service
For those of us who receive the note-taking service, we often experience it as a very complicated process. For a variety of reasons, some of us cannot take notes ourselves and have to rely on this service. At our campus, the note-taker is not assigned by the DRC, probably because of budget cuts, but instead has to be recruited in the classroom. This often results in uncomfortable situations such as the instructors publicly asking for a volunteer in class, often unintentionally outing us in front of our classmates, and/or the helpless and frustrating feeling when no one in class is willing to share her/his notes—and this is often the case even though they are all taking notes. And if there are volunteers, it sometimes takes a few days until we receive the notes—by then, the lecture has already moved on; we've already fallen behind then. Once again, another supportive service comes with a variety of challenges.

Other challenges

Restrooms and fire drills
Yes, back to bathrooms because the reader needs to know that the basic need of going to a restroom can be a challenge if the environment does not accommodate. As mentioned, some of the bathrooms at our campus are not really accessible. Though most older buildings now have larger stalls installed for people using a wheel chair (as required by law), that does not mean that individuals using a wheelchair can always easily access the stall within the restroom. In one building on campus, a person with a wheelchair or walker has to maneuver around two narrow corners and opening doors that do not have automatic door openers, so entering the "accessible" stall in that restroom is nearly impossible. Because of those obstacles, we have to use the bathroom in the library next door. This means walking or driving down the hallway to the end of the building and entering a very small claustrophobic elevator, going to the library next door, using the restroom there, coming back, using the elevator to go back up again, and walking or driving down the hallway back to the classroom. This process can take about 15

to 20 minutes from important class time. In another building, one of us received a pass to use the freight elevator because there were too many obstacles in assessing the regular elevator. Colleges and other organizations need to keep in mind that we do not expect everything to be rebuild, we are adaptable, but a few little adjustments such as installing automatic door openers would make us feel less left out, and, in the case of the freight elevator, less of an object.

Emergency evacuation drills create yet another challenge. Fire drills are intended to ensure that the staff of a building is prepared to efficiently and orderly assist all occupants to leave the building safely in the case of an emergency. However, when the emergency is a fire, using an elevator could be lethal. Of course this presents another challenge for people using a wheelchair. To deal with this situation, buildings need to be equipped with an emergency slide. Unfortunately, installing a slide is not the total solution. During a fire drill at our college, the staff of one building could not find the key for the emergency slide to evacuate a student using a wheelchair. So, the instructor left the student all by herself in the classroom while everyone else was evacuated. Another time, when the staff actually found the key and used the slide, they just left the person lying there in the grass for quite some time until someone finally assisted him back up the stairs. This demonstrates how important it is to train staff to assist ALL students in emergency evacuation situations, so no one has to endure demeaning situations like these.

Nonvisible disabilities
It is often difficult to understand what we do not see. This holds true for nonvisible disabilities as well. Bettina asked one of her students if he could explain what it means to have post traumatic stress disorder (PTSD). Here is what he wrote:

The biggest thing I have had to learn to deal with in regards to PTSD is that it is not a state of mind. It influences everything in every aspect of your life. I deployed to Afghanistan with a Marine attack helicopter squadron from March 2004 to March 2005 and spent most of that year eight miles from the Pakistan border taking rocket and mortar fire. In addition to that, I had to bury a friend who died in a helicopter crash on his way home.

Looking back now after educating myself more, I realize I was showing PTSD symptoms as soon as I got home. I spent the first week in a hotel and would wake up at the slightest noise frantically looking for my weapon, unsure where I was. Later I would frequently drink to excess sometimes to the point of not remembering things. When stress was low, I thought I would be able to manage better despite being told that I really should seek counseling. The realization that I had no idea what I was dealing with came when I started lashing out at family and friends and pushing everyone away. When I started working in jobs that took me out of working with other military veterans or active service members, I noticed that I started pulling more and more away from my coworkers. Some of this was due to people having no idea what I had gone through and some was just people who were antagonistic to my problems. Even getting counseling wasn't helping and my therapist suggested looking into a service dog for emotional support.

When we started looking into this service, we ran into our first real roadblock. Veterans Administration changed their policy about funding service dogs as emotional support for veterans. However, instead of giving up, my wife and I investigated and found Operation Freedom Paws,[1] and I am currently going through the process of obtaining a service dog from them.

Since returning from my deployment, I have made many changes to my life so I can better manage my PTSD symptoms. I use positive self-talk and know what situations to avoid. I also avoid certain movies and shows because they can trigger flashbacks and nightmares. But my biggest help has been the unending support of my friends, wife, and children.

It is not always easy to explain what it means to have a mental illness or a learning disability, but stories like these provide an important framework to illustrate that people cannot just "snap out of it" or "just work harder." The issue is much more complex than it appears, and emotional support and accommodation are crucial.

SOME MORE UNLEARNING

"If we fear mistakes, doing things wrongly, constantly evaluating ourselves, we will never make the academy a culturally diverse place where scholars and the curricula address every dimension of that difference" (hooks, 1994, p. 33).

"The academy is not paradise. But learning is a place where paradise can be created" (hooks, 1994, p. 207).

In addition to suspicion and challenges surrounding the accommodation process, we sense some instructors' misconception of what disability really means. We had some unpleasant encounters with instructors, and it appears that uncertainty, uneasiness, and inexperience in communication with each other are the culprits. For example, one of us asked her professor about how to succeed in her/his class because she spent all her time studying for the class and was still not passing.

1 http://operationfreedompaws.org

The professor said to visit her/him during office hours to set up a study plan for her. So, she did go see her/him, and the professor said, "Just put more time into this class, and study harder." This seems to suggest that the instructor was willing to help but then lacked the appropriate communication skills to initiate a productive conversation. Then, another coauthor expressed her sadness when an instructor yelled at her to get out of the office when she just wanted to discuss how to communicate better in the future. This reaction expresses frustration on the instructor's side, and the lack of faculty support and guidance on how to work with students with disabilities. Maybe, at the moment, it was easier to get rid of a "problem" than show the willingness to confront an uncomfortable situation. These examples are not about judging instructors; it is okay to make mistakes, but only if they teach us all how to change our behavior so we can work better together. The following statements might help instructors understand that students with disabilities aren't "problem students" but rather students who face unique learning challenges that may require simple, respectful, and creative solutions.

Notes to our professors

In one session, Bettina asked, "If you could say something to your instructor to better understand what disability means and how you learn, what would you say?" Here are some of our responses:

We want professors to understand that:
- We are not disabled, we just learn differently.
- We all come in different colors, and that they should not think we're not smart just because we learn not in the same way as everyone else.
- There are a variety of disabilities—visible and non-visible. If they adjust their teaching style to accommodate everyone's learning style, it will be a benefit to all students.
- We did not ask for these disabilities. They should not treat us as if we are making excuses or are falling behind on purpose.
- We need their understanding so that our learning process can be facilitated smoothly. Losing patience and lashing out at innocent students make things worse in the long run.
- Sometimes you just have to be patient—that's a virtue.

And so, the unlearning process continues. It is a combination of investing in understanding students and not being afraid of trying out new things. Change can be stressful, especially when having to change ingrained habits and attitudes. We often expect patterns, and it can initially be confusing when these expectations are not met. However, unlearning means being curious and being open to new and exciting encounters.

Some Understanding of Disability

Name _____ **Date** _____

Think about it:

1. Do these statements make you better understand the challenges students with disabilities face in the classroom? What advice would you give students/instructors to work toward better understanding?
2. How do you feel about students receiving accommodations such as extra time, a note-taker, etc.? Do you feel it's an equal playing field? Why or why not?

Action Items:

1. Take a look at the list you created in Chapter 3 about the behaviors/attitudes you would like to unlearn. Choose one item, and then initiate the unlearning process by assessing the current situation: How did you learn this behavior/attitude? How/why is it important for you to unlearn it? How does it affect you and your relationships with others? Keep these notes since we will continue with the unlearning process in the next chapter (Appendix C).

2. Go to the website of the National Alliance of Mental Illness (NAMI) at www.nami.org. Explore the website, watch a few videos, and read testimonials. What information did you find especially helpful with unlearning the concept of mental illness?

chapter 5

Some Tips on How Students and Instructors Can Create an Inclusive Environment Together

After the assessment of the current situation, the unlearning process progresses to considering what works and what does not work to create the desired inclusive academic environment. Our group discussions led us to the realization that the responsibility to create this inclusion requires a dialogic approach from students *and* instructors. This means that both sides should be welcoming the conversation and should obtain an in-depth understanding of disability regulations. Just relying on the other side can lead to confusion and miscommunication (it does not work). Resourcefulness and the willingness to invest some time are essential in ensuring a smoother process (it works!).

Title: A Tribute to Neil Armstrong, Medium: Oil on Canvas, Year: 2012, Original in Color

There are several sources available to achieve this goal. Of course, one source is this book. It provides an overview of the accommodation process and invites an open conversation. However, every school has different regulations, as we mentioned in the accommodation section, so this requires some research of the school's disability department's website and a visit to the actual center and maybe even the testing center. Plus, most centers offer a huge variety of resources online. For example, the San José State University (SJSU) Disability Resource Center (DRC) (http://www.drc.sjsu.edu/resources/index.htm) provides comprehensive guidelines, faculty resources including fast facts for faculty, and the invitation to contact a DRC counselor. In addition, another valuable source is a handbook for students that explains the services and other important information about the overall process. Both students and instructors have to take advantage of the detailed resources disability centers provide to ensure an open and constructive dialogue. If the department on your campus does not offer these types of services, we suggest encouraging them to offer at least these.

We mentioned several times that an open communication participates in creating a trusting relationship. But what does open communication mean and who initiates it? Our experiences as students with disabilities, both positive and negative, helped us to create the following sections of guidelines we feel open up communication. While our hope is that instructors will indeed read and contemplate our "*Some* Tips for Instructors" section, for our student readership, it can serve the purpose of encouraging you to develop your own lists relating to different contexts of personal or professional interests, such as improving parents–kids, employer–employee, or partner–partner relationships. For students with disabilities, our guidelines assist with identifying a helpful instructor and with tips on how to approach an instructor in a non-threatening way.

SOME TIPS FOR INSTRUCTORS

"What does it mean to listen to a voice before it is spoken? It means making space for the other, being aware of the other, paying attention to the other, honoring the other. It means not rushing to fill our students' silences with fearful speech of our own and not trying to coerce them into saying the things we want to hear. It means entering empathetically into the student's world so that he or she perceives you as someone who has the promise of being able to hear another person's truth" (Palmer, 1998, p. 46).

THE SYLLABUS

We feel that the instructor can already initiate the conversation when creating the syllabus. The syllabus—or green sheet/course schedule—already indicates the accessibility of an instructor. Including a statement that communicates the willingness to comply with the Americans with Disabilities Act (ADA) sends a message to the students about the instructor's understanding of the accommodation process. SJSU provides this standardized statement:

> ***Campus Policy in Compliance with the Americans with Disabilities Act***
> *If you need course adaptations or accommodations because of a disability, or if you need to make special arrangements in case the building must be evacuated, please make an appointment with me as soon as possible, or see me during office hours. Presidential Directive 97-03 requires that students with disabilities requesting accommodations must register with the DRC to establish a record of their disability (Disability Resource Center).*

In addition to the inclusion of this statement on the syllabus, the first class session also participates in creating a supportive classroom environment. Announcing this campus policy section in class, instead of skipping over it out of uneasiness, will make it feel like just another component of the course. It normalizes the accommodation process and indicates familiarity with the campus's disability center, and this results in us feeling more comfortable approaching faculty to ask for help.

Also, instructors should consider making their syllabi available to students before class starts, and as early as possible, so students, who use a screen reader, can ensure that they have a digital version of the textbook at the beginning of the semester. Otherwise, students might have to wait—in some cases several weeks—for its conversion (i.e., an electronic version suitable for screen readers). This lag time immediately puts us behind since we can't do the assigned readings. Our campus has a center that creates the electronic version of a textbook; they advise instructors to include the textbook's ISBN number in the syllabus since that helps them with the process.

Lesson Plans and Expectations

Often, instructors have generic expectations about students when creating lesson plans, such as: All students can read, do not mind working in groups, are mobile and can participate in kinesthetic events or outside activities, etc. However, to create a supportive classroom atmosphere, instructors should be prepared and flexible to adjust accordingly. To illustrate:

- Students using a screen reader might struggle if called on in class to read. *Some solutions:* Asking for volunteers to read. Or, using a screen reader to read to the class.
- Students diagnosed with post traumatic stress disorder or bipolar might feel extreme anxiety when having to work in groups. *Some solutions:* Announcing at the beginning of the course that the class requires group work. This allows students with concerns about this activity to contact instructors beforehand. Also, discussing group work rules, such as "invite

but do not force people to speak" and "respect each other's different viewpoints" could help.
- Students with illnesses such as asthma or fibromyalgia might not feel comfortable with kinesthetic activities or other activities performed outside the classroom. *Some solutions:* Announcing these activities beforehand, so students can prepare and/or contact the instructor. Or, creating kinesthetic group activities that include both active and administrative tasks.

These adjustments can be easily incorporated without having to drastically change lesson plans. They should not feel like a burden to the instructor but a routine consideration when preparing lessons. Actually, these adaptations will benefit every student since every student within the class learns differently. Varying methods between lectures, group activities, and kinesthetic work will also make class more engaging for everyone, and it ensures that the majority of students' learning styles are accommodated.

Accessibility of Class Material

Instructors should have all class material available electronically for students who use screen readers. However, electronic versions do not necessarily mean that they are indeed accessible. Often professors use scanned documents with annotations or poor quality copies that interfere with screen readers. Therefore, attending one of the previously-mentioned accessibility workshops would help with creating accessible documents. Electronic handouts should also be available to students before class starts. And since nowadays most campuses implement online learning management systems with a platform to centralize all course communication and material, this is the place to post handouts early. Not only do we as students with disabilities appreciate the opportunity to prepare, but probably other students, such as non-native speakers, do as well. Plus, instructors would save time in class by not having to go over every detail of the assignments during the class period. Also, having material available electronically saves a lot of paper *and* our environment.

Lectures and Presentation Software

We understand that some instructors do not see the need to employ presentation software such as *PowerPoint, Keynotes,* or *Prezi.* However, there are several advantages associated with the use of these tools. Presentation software, if used correctly, can accommodate more learning styles than lecturing alone. It provides an additional visual that helps students better remember and understand class concepts. Plus, instructors can keep their presentations organized and post them online as an additional study tool for students.

However, there are a few things to consider when using these types of software. Here are some tips for creating accessible presentations:
- Avoiding blank slide layouts but rather choosing a slide layout option (i.e., choose from themes, masters, or other templates).
- Avoiding textboxes as they can be invisible to text-to-speech software.
- Ensuring each slide has a unique title since this serves as a heading structure for the screen reader software.
- Including closed captions for any video or audio.
- Using colors with enough contrast for people with color blindness or low vision. The safest colors to use, in order: black, white, blue, yellow; colors to avoid: red and green; color combinations to avoid: red with black, red with green, blue with orange, green with magenta, yellow with cyan.
- Making font size at least 30 points. Limit bullets to three to seven per slide.
- Adding descriptions to graphics or images as the screen reader will otherwise skip them.

Bettina finds the last tip specifically helpful because she now evaluates the purpose of each image more diligently. As a result, her choice of graphics has become more meaningful and strengthens the overall message of slides. While lecturing and presenting the slides, instructors should explain each image to make them accessible to students who are blind or to those with low vision. If there really is no meaning to an image, and it was just picked because it looks nice, maybe that graphic should be deleted as it does not add value to a slide.

Remember to keep it simple! Having too many images, graphs, data, information on one slide is just confusing for everyone. It is important to remember that accessibility is for all!

We understand that some of the above mentioned requirements demand additional software proficiency skills. Schools often offer software development courses for staff and faculty. For example, at SJSU, the faculty development center offers regular *Creating Accessible Documents and Slides* workshops. The time investment to attend one of these workshops is worthwhile.

TIPS TO COMMUNICATE WITH STUDENTS WHO ARE DEAF OR HARD OF HEARING

Interpreters

In most cases, either the student or the campus's disability center will provide instructors with guidelines and requirements on how to interact with the student effectively. Most universities provide sign-language interpreters.

Since the student is the receiver of the message, it is important to talk directly to the student and not to the interpreter. This might take some time getting used to, but after a while it will just become a natural interaction. Even though interpreters cannot participate in classroom activities, they can ask for clarification when needed, and this clarification can help everyone in class. One interpreter shared that at times she has to ask instructors to repeat complicated information, so she can convey the material correctly to the student. When the instructor then tries another approach of explaining the concept, she often hears an "ahhh" from the entire class, which indicates that they also only then understood.

In addition to in-class communication, ensuring that videos, films, and all electronic media are captioned is another important aspect of ensuring an inclusive environment. If help is needed, the disability center's Deaf and Hard of Hearing Services Program provides help and contact information.

Assistive Listening Device

An assistive listening device (ALD) filters out background noises so students can hear their lectures more clearly. ALDs alleviate some of the exhaustion associated with trying to concentrate on what an instructor discusses when noise levels are really high in a classroom due to bad acoustics or other environmental sounds. The student will ask the instructor to wear a microphone that directly transmits to the student's earpiece. Usually an instructor will receive an accommodation letter from the disability center with additional guidelines and tips. To include the student into class discussions, instructors can either hand the microphone to other students who are speaking or repeat the questions and comments for the benefits of everyone in class. Once again, this might take some time getting used to, but these adjustments can be easily integrated into the classroom interaction.

COMMUNICATION IN THE CLASSROOM AND BEYOND

To arrange for a note-taker, an instructor should not announce to the entire class, "We have a student who needs a note-taker," because this does not protect our confidentiality rights. Instead, the instructor should suggest a few note-takers and then approach them privately to ask if they are willing. Most universities offer early registration for student note-takers so that might be an incentive in addition to also preparing useful and thorough notes for themselves. The instructors could also consider offering extra credit for note-takers and post the notes in an online forum or email them to the entire class as a benefit for all students. Fill-in-the-blank outlines are also a useful note-taking tool.

Furthermore, uncertainty about students' rights and faculty responsibility under federal laws and statutes may result in ineffective communication. It is often the fear of making a mistake that leads to awkward situations. Instructors and students should know that "contrary to disability legislation governing secondary schools, disability laws at the postsecondary level forbid university faculty and staff from asking a student if s/he has a disability" (Disability Resource Center, 2006, p. 4). The same applies to questions requesting details about a disability. To open the conversation about the accommodation process, we suggest questions such as: What kind of learner are you? What can I do to help you do well? How can I collaborate with the disability center to make sure you have the best possible chance of succeeding in the class?

Beyond the classroom, department chairs should serve as role models and address these ideas in department faculty meetings and/or require instructors to participate in related faculty workshops. When we feel supported by the department, we are more likely to return that support and also feel more confident when asking professors in that department to accommodate us.

Do you have additional tips for instructors? Email us to add your own tips.

SOME TIPS FOR STUDENTS

Students can also open up the conversation with their instructors. To illustrate how that might work, a student once emailed Bettina his concerns with her communication course even before the semester started. He informed her that he had developed severe post traumatic stress disorder (PTSD) after spending two years in Iraq as a Marine machine gunner. Similar to Chris who has shared some of his struggles with us before, PTSD also impacted this student's daily life activities. Because of his PTSD, he could not stand in front of crowds or groups for any period of time. Until he registered for the communication class, he had managed without filing paperwork with the DRC as his former instructors were capable of offering him alternative ways of presenting his work. However, this communication course required students to complete several public speaking presentations, so he sensed early on that this particular class would be a challenge for him. In fact, he had put this class off for that reason. His email correspondence communicated his frustration and disappointment with having to ask for special treatment. He did not want to be treated differently or be singled out, but now he found himself in the situation of having to ask for just that. He explained his PTSD this way:

I'm pretty comfortable answering whatever questions you have, even though I'm still trying to figure PTSD out myself. It's something I've only been dealing with for a couple years, and it gets progressively worse and then seemingly better at times. The main thing to understand is that my brain has been rewired—it still responds to normal situations as if I were in severe combat. In a way, it's like sometimes I'm a prisoner of my own mind because I can't completely control it. If it were simply a fear of public speaking, by all means I would be up for the challenge... I've never been the kind of person to back down from anything. But this is far more severe and complex. It's a feeling of constant hyper-vigilance, so when I think people are looking at me or staring, something clicks in my mind, and I immediately go into an almost primitive fight or flight mode. Basically it saved my ass in Iraq, and now I can't shake it.

If he had not contacted Bettina, she would have wondered why this student always showed up early for class picking the same seat in the last row and leaving class as soon as she asked students to get into groups. After his email and talking with him, she understood that he needed a direct route to the exit and would not feel comfortable having people sitting behind him (PTSD symptoms). He helped her to understand his needs, and because of his openness, they sat down together to work out a solution. As a result, this student eventually registered with SJSU's Disability Resource Center and they advised him to choose another communication course with fewer presentation events.

However, we reiterate once again that students do not have to disclose their disabilities, and the purpose of the above story is not to make anyone feel the need to do so. Rather, it demonstrates how instructor/student consultation can assist students more effectively.

Here is a checklist for students with disabilities (in addition to those provided by disability centers) to use:

- ❏ Contact the disability center as soon as you know you are transferring to a college/university. Don't wait until the last minute. Especially with the budget cuts, these centers are often understaffed and often become crowded at the beginning of a semester.
- ❏ Have copies of all your documentation prepared (e.g., doctor's note, information from previous school/college) when visiting with your counselor for the first time.
- ❏ Become familiar with the disability department's website since most offer useful and valuable resources such as guidelines, to-do lists, etc. Pay specific attention to rules and regulations since they differ among colleges.
- ❏ Take any tests you have to take as soon as you can to ensure you can register early and get into desired classes. Contact your academic advisor for

advice on your first semester and what courses to take. We do not recommend taking classes such as English and math at the same time.
- ❏ Check out websites such as ratemyprofessor.com; talk to your counselor and other students to learn more about professors, their teaching styles, and their accommodation knowledge and practices before registering for classes.
- ❏ Take all your course syllabi to your counselor as soon as possible (check online early on) for help with scheduling appointments, finding note-takers, and starting the process of writing papers.
- ❏ Schedule regular appointments with your counselor.
- ❏ Become acquainted with various resources on campus such as the student services center, the library, tutorial center, etc.
- ❏ Check if there is a student organization or club for students with disabilities. This provides support, ensures academic involvement, and allows you to connect and make friends.
- ❏ Know your rights! One of us had an instructor who denied accommodation due to a negative attitude toward our disability center. Immediately talk to your counselor in situations like these.
- ❏ Be prepared to tell your professors what you need in order to accommodate you. Simply disclosing a disability does not help the professor provide support for you, especially if the professor is not familiar with that particular disability. This is not necessarily fair, you shouldn't have to teach teachers about disability, but the more willing you are to talk about it, the more that communication can help the instructor understand how to serve other disabled students.

Do you have additional tips for students? Please email us.

SOME WISHLIST

We are dreamers, and we envision an environment that does not keep people from succeeding. Here are some ideas that we feel would help students with disabilities:
- Disability centers should provide a list of professors who have a reputation of working well with students with disabilities and who understand the accommodation process. This list should also describe the instructor's teaching style since we all learn differently and might prefer one style over the other.

- Every instructor should read this booklet, and faculty workshops on accommodation and accessibility should be mandatory.
- The disability center and/or students with disabilities club should set up a booth at the beginning of each semester to hand out information about the process. These should be inviting and welcoming booths with catchy phrases such as *Have trouble learning?*
- Offer a mentoring program, so students with disabilities who have experiences with the campus could mentor new students.
- Offer study skills classes specifically designed for students with disabilities. Usually these generalized workshops are based on research using nondisabled students and so do not strongly relate to students with disabilities.
- With standardized accommodations, campuses could communicate with one another about their accommodation programs, so students do not have to try to figure it out on their own when transferring from one college to another.

Do you want to add to this wishlist? Does your college have some of these ideas in place already? Email us to add your own ideas.

Name _____ Date _____

Think about it:

Who do you think is responsible for creating a supportive classroom environment? The instructor or the students? Or both?

Action Items:

1. Make your own wishlist as it relates to you in a personal or professional context. For example, you might write down where you want to be in five years. Then, choose one realistic and measurable wish and create an action plan how you intend to get there. Post this in a place where you can see it all the time.
2. Continue with the unlearning process: Go back and review your notes you created in Chapter 4. Now take a look at the behavior/attitude you noted and write down the things that work and that don't work, preferably in the form of a table. This enables you to analyze the behavior/attitude in further detail by thinking about how it both positively and negatively affects you and your relationships with others. As a next step, work off that table to create guidelines and tips you feel would help with moving to the next level, the level that can really initiate a change of that specific behavior/attitude. Be creative! Also post these guidelines in a place where you can see them all the time. Then start following those tips and guidelines (Appendix C).

chapter 6

Some Different Perspectives

At times, we brought in outside resources to start our conversation. The following NPR broadcast featuring Ben Mattlin exhibited a new and radical perspective about disability that some of us hadn't considered before, so we decided to think more about it and did not respond immediately. Then, a few days later, Vashti emailed her response as a different perspective to Ben Mattlin's comments.

Ben Mattlin:
I get a lot of recommendations to join Facebook groups with names like Fight SMA. I never respond.

SMA stands for spinal muscular atrophy, and I was born with it. I've never walked or stood, and over time have lost the use of my hands. It's a progressive neuromuscular weakness. It occurs in one of every 6,000 births, and is the most common cause of genetically-based neonatal death. So fighting it is a noble cause, and I feel for parents who've lost their babies, but it's not my cause. I can never support a group that aims to cure me.

My disability is part of who I am. It's all I've ever known. Who would I be without it? It doesn't define me, but it has informed every aspect of my life. Even as a child, I never dreamed of walking. Flying, yes. I wanted to be a superhero, but I never wanted to be just like everyone else.

My big brother, who doesn't have SMA, once asked me what I'd do if there were an operation that could fix my muscles but risked leaving me worse off or dead. No thanks, I said. Even then, it was the thought of losing my trademark wheels that terrified me, not death.

© 2010 Ben Mattlin. NPR® news commentary titled "*Spinal Muscular Atrophy 'Doesn't Define Me*" by Commentator Ben Mattlin was originally broadcast on NPR's Morning Edition® on April 28, 2010, and is used with the permission of NPR. Any unauthorized duplication is strictly prohibited.

I can see that being able to do more physically would be helpful. I'd like to be a little less dependent on other people and machinery. But when I try to picture myself stripped of my disability, it leaves me feeling cold and lost. My Facebook friends might not agree. Many people with SMA do feel more physically vulnerable than I do. Yes, I know I wouldn't be here without scientific progress.

Yet I can't help having a mental block against medicalizing disability. It just doesn't square with my particular form of disability pride. After all, if you dream of a cure, aren't you saying we're not okay as we are? And if we focus on medical fixes, don't we risk misdirecting our energies away from the external inequities that we can and must end: the barriers of architecture, attitudes and economics that truly handicap us?

Disability is a fact of life. It's here to stay, so why not celebrate it as another part of human diversity? Call me crazy, but I sort of like myself just the way I am.

Vashti's response:
I do not know who I would be without my disability (multiple sclerosis). It has made me appreciate life more than I did before my disability. I cannot say that I do not pray for a cure, because I do. It is not about being like everyone else, but I would love to be able to do the things that I used to do, like long distance running. I do not agree that dreaming of a cure means that we are saying that we are not okay. I think it's a sign of strength, and hope. I know my life will be great with or without a cure because I have accepted my disability. I also know that many who are diagnosed are not strong enough to handle it. The search for a cure gives people hope, which sometimes, is all we have. I support any efforts to cure multiple sclerosis because I saw what my mother went through as a result of this disability, and if I can do something to stop others from having to go through this, I will.

Bettina's response:
I understand both perspectives, and we do not have to take sides here or choose one over the other. Personally, the broadcast made me contemplate my own attitude toward disability and my own fear about becoming disabled someday, and there is a high chance that most of us will at some point in our lives. I believe that this dysfunctionphobia is embedded in a lot of people's mind. But working with people with disabilities has shown me that it is often the environment that disables, and that discourse also participates in creating negative attitudes toward the term disability. One narrative that contributes to this

negativism idea is the "overcoming narrative." In this narrative, we hear heroic stories of people "overcoming" their disability, which implies that disability is something that should be overcome. Here, Ben Mattlin's story makes sense because he does not believe he needs to overcome anything. He is probably correct that these overcoming stories communicate that being different is undesirable, and that we should do everything possible to be "normal." If society, if we, would communicate more openly and differently about disability, we could lessen dysfunctionphobia and the desire to always fit in.

Certainly, this project has definitely changed my perspective about disability. My coauthors have taught me a lot, and the interaction with them made me a more well-rounded person. They not only helped me see beautiful things I haven't seen before, but they also helped me recognize barriers that participate in the creation of disability. For example, while traveling in London and using the underground, my partner and I had to carry our heavy luggage up and down the stairs as most stations did not have an elevator. I immediately thought of how people using a wheel chair would get around in this inaccessible environment. I checked the underground website and found the information that only a few stations were accessible (but *Transport for London* is working diligently to improve this situation).[1] I am sure that other people besides people with disabilities would appreciate a more accessible public transportation system because we came across lots of people huffing and puffing while dragging heavy loads across the many steps… Of course, this book will not have the power to transform the massive London underground system, but it can start us all thinking about ways to create an environment that enables rather than disables.

SOME STARTING THE CONVERSATION

When asking friends and colleagues to provide feedback on the book, we were delighted that some immediately engaged in the conversation. As this is a book in progress that will grow with readers' input, we decided to already include Dana's response here as well:

> Mr. Mattlin, Vashti, and Bettina,
> I enjoyed all your remarks about disability. I would, however, like to add a few notes to your discussion. Often in studies of disability, those of us who

[1] http://www.tfl.gov.uk/corporate/projectsandschemes/5792.aspx

have any kind of disability are lumped into the same category despite our different and unique needs. I am learning disabled, but I get my accommodations from the same place that both Mr. Mattlin and Vashti would go for their accommodations.

I think what makes disability part of our identity is how we embody it. My disability, for lack of a better term, is in my head and there is no cure for me, there never will be. I'm also reminded of my fellow disabled students who have distinctly different disabilities, but who also have no hope for a cure; people with bi-polar disorder, traumatic brain injury, and fibromyalgia, to name a few.

Is it wrong to hope for a cure for what ails you? Only the individual can answer that question. At one time, I hoped for a cure for my own disability, but soon realized it was holding me back in my own life. Once I accepted my limitations, I gained a tremendous amount of freedom. I still struggle with self-acceptance from time to time, despite being in my thirties. It's hard knowing you are drastically different from your peers.

To me, it's not important whether or not you secretly wish, openly desire, or publicly work toward a cure, it's what you do with your identity as a disabled person (temporary or permanent), how you help others (disabled or not), and how you help yourself that matters in the long run. Because for this time, long or short, we are all united in our limitations, brothers and sisters in disability, who should be helping one another.

Some Different Perspectives 51

Name _____ **Date** _____

Think about it:

If there were something you could change about yourself, what would it be? Do you think you would still be the same person? Why or why not?

Action item:

Find an article with which you completely disagree. Read it with an open mind and write a list of the points, expressions, and statements you agree with and/or at least could tolerate. How did this change your overall initial attitude toward this writing?

chapter 7

Some Life Beyond Academia

"Stop with the labels ... because we are not jam jars; we are extraordinary, different, wonderful people" (Caroline Casey).

Title: The Land Of, Medium: Oil on Canvas, Year: 2010, Original in Color

Courtesy of Jesse Molina

This chapter features a combination of our discussions, experiences, research, conversations with employers and employees, and our vision of an inclusive work environment. We decided to incorporate more outside sources due to our, until now, limited experiences within the job market. Therefore, this chapter exhibits a slightly different voice than previous chapters; however, this voice still represents us, and we enjoyed the integration of a variety of meaningful information.

SOME TRANSITION

Now that some of us have graduated or are close to graduating, we find ourselves, like every other graduate, in a competitive labor environment searching for jobs. For people with disabilities, the prospect of finding a job is even more difficult. According to the Bureau of Labor Statistics (BLS), the unemployment rate for people with disabilities was 15 percent in 2011, higher than the rate for those with no disability at 8.7 percent (U.S. Department of Labor Statistics, 2012).

The support we received in the academic environment assisted us with pursuing a degree, and this book demonstrates that achieving our goals required persistence, flexibility, hard work, and constantly fighting the stigma associated with having a disability. Now the received accommodations might work against us because of misconceptions of what these accommodations entail. The suspicion that a person received "too much support" or "took advantage of the system," coupled with a general lack of knowledge about the work skills of people with disabilities, might deter employers from hiring a person with a disability.

This chapter is geared toward counteracting these suspicions. To clarify, the labor market does not endow advantages to people with disabilities. Except for some federal agencies, there is no distinct requirement for corporations in the United States to hire people with disabilities. The Americans with Disabilities Act (ADA), signed into law in 1990, can only do so much. According to Title I of the ADA, employers with fifteen or more employees have "to provide qualified individuals with disabilities an equal opportunity to benefit from the full range of employment-related opportunities available to others. For example, it prohibits discrimination in recruitment, hiring, promotions, training, pay, social activities, and other privileges of employment" (U.S. Department of Justice, 2009). However, it is up to the discretion of the employer to define "qualified."

Here it becomes tricky. Should an applicant reveal his/her disability in the application and/or interview? Title I of the ADA restricts questions that can be asked about an applicant's disability status, but what would you do if you were asked? Most of us would not, and in some cases did not, reveal our disability because we worried that this would render us "disqualified" in the eyes of the employer. Of course, for those of us with non-visible disabilities, it is much easier to "hide" our disability than for those of us using a walker or wheel chair. We are aware that some employers might have negative preconceptions about work skills of people with disabilities and will avoid hiring us if they don't have to. A recent study by the Confederation of German Trade Unions (DGB) confirms this concern: 60 percent of German employers do not follow their required employment of people with disabilities but rather pay a penalty charge of 290 Euro per noncovered quota (El-Sharif, 2012). The study blames in part the ignorance of the private economy. In the United States, the ADA is supposed to counteract similar sentiments, but as Braithwaite and Labrecque (1994) state, "[A]lthough legislation can address physical access and removal of employment barriers, it is not possible to legislate beliefs, attitudes, and behaviors toward persons with disabilities"(p. 289). So, our goal is, once again, to help the reader change beliefs, attitudes, and behaviors to foster an understanding of people with disabilities and to decrease uncertainty how to interact.

SOME BENEFITS OF INCLUDING DISABILITY INTO COMPANY PRACTICES (WORKING *WITH*)

Consumers respond positively to socially responsible companies. In addition to the widely accepted social responsibility standard of sustainability, recently accessibility has evolved as an additional valuable standard. Now companies can also pride themselves for being one of the top companies for people with disabilities[1] or for having received the Helen Keller Award by the American Association of the Blind.[2] These awards and recognitions enhance a company's image and with it the bottom line. Since the term "bottom line" has commonly only factored in financial gain, we want to borrow sustainability's three pillars of the triple bottom line: people, planet, profit. This concept encourages corporations to measure their success by not only monetary standards but by social and environmental standards as well. This balanced approach will ensure a company's longevity by incorporating responsible business strategies.

SOME PEOPLE

This pillar provides a framework for equitable company practices ensuring the welfare of all employees. For us, this means that companies should not shy away from hiring people with disabilities because of unfounded concerns. As previously mentioned, it is often uncertainty and ignorance that prevents employers from hiring people with disabilities. Disability staffing companies such as Opportunity Works and The Sea Glass Group offer a one-to-one approach to help companies understand the benefits of employing people with disabilities. Another example is the company *Specialisterne*, Danish for "the specialists." Inspired by the skills of his son, who was diagnosed with autism, a Danish father founded the company employing workers with autism who are hired out as consultants for tasks such as data entry or software testing. The father, Thorkil Sonne, states, "given the right environment, an autistic adult could not just hold down a job but also be the best person for it" (Cook, 2012). The German software company SAP started working with *Specialisterne* to employ people with autism on a global level.[3] We suggest companies following this lead and seeking out disability staffing companies to tap into the pool of talented and

---

1 http://www.diversityinc.com/diversity-management/the-diversityinc-top-10-companies-for-people-with-disabilities-2/
2 http://www.afb.org/section.aspx?FolderID=1&SectionID=28&TopicID=152&DocumentID=1595
3 http://www.reuters.com/article/2013/05/22/us-sap-autism-idUSBRE94L0ZN20130522

well-educated people with disabilities. We do not want to be hired because of our disability but because we are the most qualified person for the position.

To give us a chance requires an open mind. Here people often address the concept of empathy. However, we feel that (just) developing empathy is not always sufficient. Let us clarify this sentiment. Empathy is defined as the ability to understand and share the feelings of another., but we wonder if it is indeed possible to *share* with others our entire experiences and emotions of what it means to live with a disability. People often learn to empathize when they suddenly find themselves in a similar situation. For example, people shared with us that only after having to use crutches because of an injury, did they realize the inaccessibility of their environment (e.g., lack of automatic door opener). We overall value the concept of empathy, but experiences such as these do not ensure a *real* understanding of what a person with a disability experiences or feels. We should not impose attitudes and feelings on others just from the perspective of a limited viewpoint or experience. Actually, some of the issues with disability in the workforce are due to the preconceived notion of what a person with a disability should be like and/or feel like.

Instead, starting a conversation is a more effective tool to learn about our qualifications. For example, a new CEO at a small company asked his employees to introduce themselves through a medium of their choice such as creating a video, a PowerPoint or Keynote presentation, an audio recording, or writing an email. The new CEO not only learned about his new team and their work responsibilities, experiences, and education, but was also able to identify strengths of each employee. After consulting with them, he then assigned tasks considering the talents of each employee. And, it is ok to ask questions such as: What can I do to best support you and to understand your working style? What do you need from me/us to do your job effectively? Yes, because these are constructive questions geared toward all employees.

Some Planet (the work environment)

For this pillar, we are considering the underlying concept of environment, the physical and social work environment.

Some physical environment

An accessible environment should of course consist of a legally constructed building which incorporates accessibility standards such as ramps and automatic door openers[4] in addition to a wide variety of accessible software such as screen reader software to create an overall inclusive work environment.

---

4 http://www.access-board.gov/adaag/html/adaag.htm

In this context of a physical environment, we again want to mention the accessibility of bathrooms. In addition to inaccessibility of bathrooms in older buildings, accessing newer wider stalls designed for people using a walker or wheelchair can also be problematic. In one conversation, we talked about how often these stalls were taken by people who do not really need the larger space. We ask others to reserve this stall for people with disabilities as a way of showing respect and an understanding of our needs. No need to feel guilty here, Bettina was one of these people, as well.

Some social environment
Including disability management in employee and/or diversity training is an effective strategy to create an inclusive work environment. This strategy also conveys social responsibility and well-rounded business practices. There are a number of communication consultants who focus on this topic and offer innovative approaches, so we encourage employers to hire one of these experienced consultants. The inclusion of the topic of accessibility and disability can have a number of positive effects. For one, it decreases uncertainty how to communicate with people who are different from us and allows for more relaxed, open, compassionate, and productive interaction within a team. It also increases the understanding of disabilities and decreases stigma associated with it. As that, it creates a positive workplace climate.

Plus, the inclusion of the topic of accessibility and disability shows employees that the company supports individuals with disabilities, so they might be more open to seek help if they themselves perceive some mental health issues such as depression or feelings of being burned out. In the United States alone, depression causes about 200 million lost workdays each year at a cost of $44 billion to employers (Stewart, Ricci, Chee, Hahn, & Morganstein, 2003), so the earlier employees ask for help and receive treatment and support, the earlier they can continue being productive team members; and thus, this would also take care of the next pillar: *profit*.

SOME PROFIT

To fulfill its commitment to employees, a company cannot neglect its obligation to gain profit. That being said, though, hiring people with disabilities can provide companies with a new competitive edge because it connects the company with a huge number of potential customers with disabilities. Remember, people with disabilities are the largest minority group in the world. Add in related family members, friends, and caregivers, and there is an even larger group of people interested in companies that focus on accessibility. Any resulting company message, of course, will be perceived as more honest and realistic if it was created in cooperation with people with disabilities because people with disabilities have the required experience to connect with an audience of similar experience. The idea is similar to this book and the concept of writing *with* and not *about*.

Of course, not only does employing people with disabilities help businesses connect with a broader audience, it also increases the number of creative and out-of-the-box thinkers involved in the inner workings of that business. Disabilities demand us to be problem solvers, and this transfers into job skills.[5] Our disabilities have definitely taught us to be hard workers, to be creative, and resilient. The Chicagoland Chamber of Commerce's disabilityworks conducted a costs and benefits study which determined that "employers benefitted from dedicated and reliable employees and a diverse workforce" (Hernandez & McDonald, 2008). They found that there were not any major differences regarding supervision or job performance, and employers with disabilities were not absent as often as those employees without disabilities. Furthermore, this study found that there are no risks associated with hiring people with disabilities but only benefits, so a truly diverse team should not exclude people with disabilities.

What do you think: Are the three pillars of sustainability applicable to the unlearning of the concept of disability?

SOME TIPS FOR PEOPLE WITH DISABILITIES TRYING TO ENTER THE JOB MARKET

When Bettina asked about tips to include in the book for people with disabilities trying to enter the job market, some of us had an insightful discussion we would like to share with you. However, we want to add a disclaimer. These are our thoughts, and we do not want to offend anyone who has a different opinion and/or attitude. We are aware that there are a number of people with disabilities out there who have experiences that we have not addressed in our discussion. These words are meant to help unlearn our own concept of disability and to fight the aforementioned generalizations about people with disabilities in the workforce. "If you do not have thick skin, do not read it. My disability gave me thick skin, and sugarcoating things doesn't work for me (Vashti)."

---

5 http://www.workwithoutlimits.org/employers/sense/workplace

Don't allow your disability to be your own roadblock. Do not tell yourself, I want this job, but they will not hire me because of my disability. Focus on the things you can do and not on the ones you can't. If you carry your weaknesses with you inside yourself, everyone can see them. If you focus too much on your disability, you might see it as an entitlement: They owe this to me. And that attitude will reflect negatively on your identity. You have to be the best candidate for the position. If you are not, you shouldn't get the job "just" because you have a disability. It is not your fault that you have a disability, but what you do with it is. Do not make yourself the victim. Do not blame others but take responsibility for your own actions. The disability is outside your control, so focus on the things you are in control of. If you always blame the world for your problems, you do not get anywhere. It is a very individualistic world. If someone discriminates against you, push harder. If you don't get the job you applied for, do not whine and look for a different job. Do not live in the past. Move on to do something different. Complaining doesn't help. We like getting things done.

To be honest, some of us are disheartened and frustrated due to the lack of employment. But we know that these feelings do not only ring true for people with disabilities. Getting together to talk about our struggles and challenges helps. And sometimes harsher words, as shared above, push us to work even harder. We are very resilient, but we still want to contribute to society and hope that we will get a chance soon.

Here are some additional tips we discussed in our meetings:

- During your time in college, make sure to volunteer and to apply for an internship. These activities will not only provide relevant work skills but will also help with expanding your network.
- To compensate for the lack of work experience on your resume, in addition to volunteer work and internships, list relevant course projects as well.
- Use your college's career center. Some of us participated in workshops on creating resumes, on solidifying elevator pitches, and on practicing interviewing skills.
- Connect with the Department of Rehabilitation[6] and WorkAbility[7] early on as well as with employment agencies. Search the web to find the agency closest to you. The ones we worked with are Work2Future, Nova Career Center, Manpower, Office Team, and Apple One

---

6 http://www.rehab.cahwnet.gov
7 http://www.cde.ca.gov/sp/se/sr/wrkabltyI.asp

- By the way, the Department of Rehabilitation also offers useful workshops and supporting groups. These are additional avenues to strengthen your network.
- Stay in contact with instructors you had a good relationship with, so they can be your reference when applying for jobs.
- While you're looking for jobs, do not get discouraged if it takes longer. Try to stay productive by volunteering, attending workshops, and updating your resume.

Well, this is definitely a chapter to be continued! Some of us are still in the process of trying to find a job, and we wish we could have contributed even more to the discussions. But we are optimistic that for the third edition, we will have more experiences and insights to share about the work environment.

Name _____ Date _____

Action items:

1. Take a look at the top ten companies for people with disabilities (see link below). Then choose one company and explore the company website on how this corporation includes accessibility and disability. http://www.diversityinc.com/diversity-management/the-diversityinc-top-10-companies-for-people-with-disabilities-2/

2. Make a list of your specific skills-set such as education, qualifications, experiences, etc.—similar to a *summary of qualifications* section on a resume. Using employment websites such as monster.com or careerbuilder.com, search for job postings that align well with your skills by typing in keywords (e.g., German language, graphic design). Choose three job titles that seem to be a good fit. Now imagine you are preparing for a job interview: Choose at least three sentences/requirements stated in the job posting for which you could readily demonstrate that you are the right, most qualified person for the job. How would you argue your case? Which experiences and qualifications would you highlight?

   Next, choose three sentences/requirements from job postings for which you do not have the qualifications, yet. How would you address these in an interview? Consider exploring transferable skills and/or experiences that highlight how you can adjust to challenges. Or, do you feel that these requirements are necessary skills that ensure a good job performance? Would you apply for that job anyway or search for different options?

chapter 8

Some Closure

"A story is not a story until it is told; it is not told until it is heard; once it is heard, it changes—and becomes open to the beauties and frailties of more change" (Pollock, 2006, p. 93).

The idea of "closure" does not fit well at this point because this second edition should encourage a continuous dialogue. However, we must "wrap up" book two at this point so book three can begin. We want to thank everyone who already participated in the conversations inspired by the first edition. Your contributions have enriched this second edition, and our hope is that this book continues improving the lives of students and employers/employees who are labeled "different."

In addition, our hopes are that this book carries on the idea of taking a new direction by understanding that differences mean opportunity; that we can collectively change the academic and work environment so that instead of students and employers/employees fearing to disclose their disability, they feel confident enough to share it as easily as their major or education; that our language choices and our behaviors convey respect; and that everyone is willing to engage in a dialogic process that focuses on solutions.

We understand that the road taking us to the realization of these hopes can be rocky, and that is okay. Life with a disability is hard, but it would be harder for us to give up. We *also* have to unlearn the concept of disability. As a process, a journey, we are aware that we might never reach *the* final destination, which is okay, too. As long as we move forward along the road, do not stop and do not go backwards, we will welcome the ups and downs. So do not be afraid. Feel free to share your doubts and troubles, but do not forget to include your hopes and dreams as well. We are looking forward to hearing from you.

Some Closure

Name _____ **Date** _____

Think about it:

What does the word *disability* evoke in you? Without evaluation and any contemplation, quickly write down thoughts and feelings you associate with this word.

Compare this list to the one generated at the beginning of the book. Has your perception changed? How has it changed? If it has changed, which parts of the book helped you with gaining a different perspective? If it hasn't changed: What's missing? What questions did we leave uncovered? Your feedback is welcome in developing an even better resource for students and instructors in the future.

This is not the end, this is
THE BEGINNING

Appendix A

Some Coauthors

Here is where you are going to meet some of the incredible coauthors of this book. Zenon will hopefully share her stories in a future edition.

ANDREW

I am Andrew Arredondo, a Communication Studies major studying at San José State University (SJSU). At birth, the physicians who assisted my mother in giving me life were the same doctors who conducted tests on me and diagnosed me with having autism. The doctors nonchalantly deduced to my parents that because of my condition they should not expect me to go to school, let alone an institution of higher learning. Apparently, the doctors at the same hospital where I was born underestimated my potential after labeling me autistic. That warranted them in categorizing me as mentally inferior because of my disability. They really thought that I would never possess the mental capacity and capability to learn anything concrete in the classroom. From K-12, I was part of the Special Education program, and eventually, I was transitioned into regular classes. Because I was mainstreamed, I always thought of myself as a typical child who wanted to do things as much as the other children were doing. I have always been a shy and somewhat awkward person who has been a target of both criticism and ridicule. My father, on the other hand, always believed in me. Thereby, he instilled in me the love of learning. I remember that he would sit with me and read the newspaper to me. It was in these special learning moments that I began to pick up information through newspapers, books, magazines, television, and other people. These were powerful father and son interactive times that had an impact on my learning abilities. Due to hard work and perseverance, I finally made it to SJSU despite being poor, not academically gifted, and a minority. I chose higher education to surpass others' expectations of me. My American Dream is to graduate from college with a Communication Studies degree. (Andrew graduated in May 2011. Congratulations, Andrew! Throughout his studies, he received a variety of honor awards.)

Life after graduation

Since I graduated, I have been working diligently to get a foothold in the job market. I always had plans to broaden my education beyond the baccalaureate level. Believe me, I have every intention of going to graduate school, but right now I have been looking for work, so that I have some work experience under me when I attend graduate school. I have to tell you it is rough. Competition is fierce. More people with education are fighting for very few jobs. While we endure daily rejection, we are getting further behind in the socioeconomic level. Despair sets in, and you start questioning your self-worth even though you never took shortcuts while in school to get results, it doesn't necessarily translate to the real world. I came to the realization that it all depends on who you know through smart networking and landing that internship while in school to at least get ahead in your chosen career path. In the meantime, I have been utilizing the resources of WorkAbility IV, the Department of Rehabilitation, and various employment agencies to help me along my career journey. On my end, I've been applying online to various jobs via Monster, Career Builder, Bright, and Craig's List and getting some interviews. Although I have yet to be offered a position, I learn something each time, which greatly improves my interviewing skills. To make myself more marketable, I also take advantage of free employment-based workshops offered by the same organizations that I belong to. For example, the Department of Rehabilitation offers an extensive job club workshop every week that lasts for over two hours, complete with a PowerPoint presentation and check-in at the end with each of us announcing whether our weekly goals were met, setting goals for the following week, and practicing our one-minute commercials.

CHRIS (JOINED US FOR THE SECOND EDITION)

My name is Christopher Ramirez. I am a 34-year-old veteran with post traumatic stress disorder (PTSD) related to my service in Afghanistan. As an 11-

year veteran of the Marine Corps, PTSD initially was something people were diagnosed with who couldn't handle trying to reintegrate into their families after deploying. When I got home, I thought I was fine, but noticed I couldn't sleep well and the slightest noise woke me up. I would tense up and be ready to fight when fireworks went off and could not sit in a restaurant without facing the door. I seemed to be always ready for something to happen and very little in my life was pleasing, like I was going through everything on autopilot. To this day people keep telling me that PTSD is a normal reaction to an abnormal situation, but sometimes I just feel like I am out of control of my emotions and feelings. But I have resolved that I am not going to let my PTSD define me and rule my life. When I want to withdraw and not deal with something, I instead try to find a new way to go forward. It's not an easy process and without the support I have gotten from friends and family it would seem nearly impossible. I keep persevering, and this makes PTSD a more manageable aspect of my life.

GIA

I was 26 years old when I found out I had a learning disability. I was sad to know I had one because of the stigma associated with it. I wasn't born with a learning disability; it was caused by a head trauma accident. When I was 2 years old, I was in an accident that left me unconscious for about 12 hours. Doctors told my mother that I had a 50 percent chance of living and a 50 percent chance of being in a vegetative state. Against all odds I woke up and went home the next day. Test concluded that I did not have any long-lasting effects of the trauma. In school I was never in special education. I had an elementary and junior high teacher request that I get tested for a learning disability. I got tested twice, and both times they came out saying I didn't have one. I got average grades in school, but I struggled with writing and memorization. Finally in junior college, after being tested again, I learned I have a visual learning disability. I rarely tell people I have a learning disability because I know the social stigma it presents. I am grateful for the DRC at San Jose State University—their services are great. I have one more semester at State. I don't know what my future holds for me, but I hope when the time comes and I reveal my disability to future employers, that they don't discriminate against me. It's not easy having a learning disability; our brains work different. I don't want people to feel sorry for me, but I want them to understand and accept my disability.

Thank you,
Gia

Jesse

Having a learning disability never stopped me from getting to where I am today. It has taken me many years of hard work, a lot of patience, and encouragement from others to help me to succeed in life. It was not until I was in college that I discovered I had a learning disability. Most children nowadays are identified as having a learning disability very early on and most parents want to get their child as much help as they can. However, back when I was in school, my difficulty with learning certain things was viewed as me just not trying hard enough or caring about learning, and so I just struggled through my school years frustrated that I had so much difficulty understanding and doing certain things. Just because you have a learning disability does not mean that you cannot learn or that you cannot continue your education past high school. It just means that you learn in a different way and that you may need "accommodations" in order to understand and perform.

Title: Self Portrait, Medium: Oil on Canvas, Original in Color

Courtesy of Jesse Molina

After finishing my A.A. at a community college, I was accepted to San José State University. I knew I would continue to need help in order to succeed in all my courses, so I utilized the Disability Resource Center on campus. This resource helped me acquire all the services I needed as a student with a learning disability: a note-taker and extra time on my exams were just some of the accommodations I had a right to use. I also always promptly and directly informed my professors of my learning disability and of the accommodations that I would need and most of my professors were very understanding and supportive.

School was a long and sometimes difficult journey, but I was determined to graduate and receive my diploma. In May of 2010, my determination paid off: I, Jesse Molina, became a graduate of San José State University with a B.A. in Art. What I learned from my experience: Never doubt yourself or let another individual give you doubts about your ability to accomplish something. With hard work, confidence, and perseverance you can and will reach your goal—no matter what kind of learner you are.

LuLu

My name is LuLu. When I started this project, I was in the final semester at SJSU. I got my B.A. in Child and Adolescent Development. I went on to get my Multiple Subject Teaching credential in the following year from the same institution. In the fall, I am teaching first grade in a local San Jose school. I am also a person with a disability—the specific learning disability, dyslexia. I joined this project because special education and mainstreaming in public schools has been a factor in my career from when I began volunteering two years ago. I felt it was important to do my part in spreading understanding about disabilities in the educational field, not just at the college level but elementary and high school levels. It is my personal goal to create a learning environment where all children feel safe to explore and expand their educational horizons.

When I was in kindergarten, my mom went to the school board and petitioned for my right to be tested. The school board didn't believe her. In the school board's defense, a student's ability to read and their understanding of phonics expands greatly from kindergarten to first grade. In my mother's defense, she's a mother. During elementary school, I did extra tutoring for reading and my parents have held me to high, but reasonable, educational standards. Then in the summer before I began high school, my parents took me to a psychologist. I went in with no labels and came out with a permanent one. After I qualified for accommodations, I was able to calm down when taking tests and lose the feeling of being rushed. When I reached college, I began to study my disability in depth and understand learning in general. It has and continues to fuel my love of teaching. My dyslexia has taught me so much that I really feel more abled by it than disabled.

Thank you for reading and taking that next step to creating a worldwide and more understanding learning environment.

Lulu

A first-grade teacher who also happens to be dyslexic

Vashti

My name is Vashti. I am a master's student in Nutrition and Food Science at SJSU. I was diagnosed with multiple sclerosis (MS) when I was 17. I was running track and my eyes became blurry to the point where I could not recognize people. My biggest fear growing up was that I would be diagnosed with

MS, like my mother. I was in denial for so long. I did not even tell my closest friends. I was embarrassed. People thought I was high or drunk when I would walk, and I would just laugh. It was not until I had to rely on a cane/walker that I was forced to tell. That was the hardest thing I ever had to do. I felt like I was admitting to the world that I was weak, vulnerable. I could no longer be the party girl, athlete that I used to be. It took years of isolation and mood swings for me to finally accept that I am who I am. I did not do anything to bring on this disability, so I should not be hard on myself for it.

I still have days where I wish that this was all a dream, and I would wake up and be "normal." I would not have to deal with the sorrowful looks I get. Truthfully, all in all, I do not feel sorry for myself. I would be a different person without my disability. I would have less compassion for others. I think my disability has encouraged my desire to help others. I am nicer, and my faith in God is stronger. I pray for a cure every night, but I know I will be okay if it never comes. I wish that I could let people know that in my heart, I am okay. I do not want to be pushed aside because of my MS. It makes me feel like I do not belong. I am just like everyone else, except I walk a little slower. I want people to stop labeling me "handicapped" and instead treat me like everyone else. I am a very open-minded, capable woman. I like frogs, and I get a thrill on airplanes and roller coaster rides. I sleep with my television on and crave coffee. I laugh at jokes that are not funny. People will never truly know me if they cannot see beyond my disability.

Life after the first edition

Since working on the book, my confidence in my disability has increased. Coming together with students who have gone through similar struggles has helped me to further see that I am not alone on this campus. I am only in two classes during my last semester, which has given me the time to pursue my hobbies. I am a member of at least three campus clubs. In my years here, I was accepted into the clubs without feeling as I was being judged. I feel so blessed that God gave me the courage to venture out and get involved at the school. Having a disability sometimes can dampen my spirits, but being active and involved helps brighten my day. I encourage any student to explore on-campus activities and clubs if possible. Not only can you broaden your social network, but you can also improve your college experience.

Going into the job market is daunting, but I have not had any negative experiences relating to my disability. I have tried to be as active as possible, and feel like my disability is pushing me to do more activities than most people that

I know. I will begin my dietetic internship this summer, and I am currently working with a network marketing company. I love where my life is heading, and hope that I can help inspire other students with or without disabilities in the future.

YADIRA

My name is Yadira, and I am a senior at SJSU, majoring in Nutrition Science. I will graduate next spring 2012—yeah! I am the mother of three wonderful children, and they have been my motivation and strength in life. I feel like my disabilities (not visible) have given me the courage to be persistent. I have to work much harder in order to be at the same level as the rest of my peers, and I have to ask the same questions over and over until I can process the information. I hate when people look at me and say: but, you look fine to me… I don't understand what they mean; just because my disabilities are not visible, does not mean that I do not have many difficulties. So, I tell them that, well, attention deficit disorder (ADD) is not visible. Many great people have the same disability as me, and they all succeeded in life. Our Disability Resource Center has a poster with famous people who have/had ADD such as John F. Kennedy, Michael Jordan, Bill Gates, Ludwig van Beethoven, Albert Einstein, and many more.

I have come to terms with my limitations, and always stay positive and challenge myself to become the best I can be. I visualize my future as a productive person and an example for my three children who also have ADD. I have become unsinkable, and I want to let my children know that disabilities are obstacles but should not deter them to do whatever they desire to do in life.

Life after the first edition

My years in college were long and stressful—but also fun and full of dreams. My life *after* college has also been fun because I finally do not have to study for exams or work on time-consuming assignments anymore. It has been stressful because one year after graduating, I am on the unemployment boat like many new graduates. I have had a few interviews. In addition to the nervousness I felt during the interview process, in the back of my mind I also prayed that nobody would ask me questions that would have me reveal my disabilities. I have always been scared that I would not get the job because of my disabilities. I started doubting myself if I would be able to carry on with the demands of the job market. At times I feel that the dreams I had in college were too idealistic. After college, my dreams changed from idealistic to realistic. The truth is that I do not have the job that I thought I would be having by now. However, the extra time helps me to prepare more intensively for the state certification exam I am planning to take soon (the silver lining...).

Another dream I have is to travel around the world. Now that my children are older, my wings are stronger, and I am ready to "fly." I want my wings to take me to places, such as Germany, and meet all of you who are now reading my brief story. Please take the time and sit down to share your own stories. I want to thank you because if it were not for you and this second edition, I would have never had the opportunity to share my frustrations and dreams. I might not be employed yet here in California, but I know that my real mission in this world has not yet been fulfilled. I love you all. Yadira

Bettina (editor/coauthor)

Hello, my name is Bettina, and I had the pleasure of listening to my coauthors' experiences as students with disabilities in higher education as well as job seekers in a competitive market (for the second edition). My job was to assemble their, which became our, stories in a cohesive manner. When we met for the first time, I was in my last semester of graduate school working on completing my Master's in Communication Studies. I could not imagine a more rewarding way of concluding my studies at SJSU than working with these talented people. I always struggled with the idea of working with a community/culture to which I do not belong, and I struggled with how this would affect my credibility. However, I quickly realized that by categorizing myself as being non-disabled, I instantly excluded myself from this amazing community. My coauthors never made me feel like an outsider, and even though I have never experienced their stories directly, they helped me to make sense of them. Of course, I am sure that my non-disabled privilege and perspective sneaked also into this second edition, and that some of my bridging thoughts might not adequately conjoin all coauthors' experiences and feelings. However, on this endeavor, we worked *with* one another to ensure that we all could agree with the overall messages.

Life after the first edition

Life after the first edition has been adventurous and at times a bit overwhelming. After the excitement of completing the first edition subsided, everyday life took over. As a lecturer teaching communication courses at three institutions, it was challenging to juggle all responsibilities while still continuing meaningful and substantial conversations surrounding disability. I spoke and taught at German universities about inclusion and academia, and these assignments demanded continued research and education on my side. However, I felt detached and wondered if I was still working *with*. I missed and needed my coauthors' inspiration and guidance! I asked them if they would be interested in working on a second edition. They promptly agreed, and our conversations provided me with the energy to take on this project once more. This time it was a bit more challenging to cohesively collaborate as we were not all attending the same university anymore, but we were able to connect online to create what you hear or see right now. I hope you find our additions and revisions meaningful!

appendix B

Timer _____ / Seat _____

Fall 2011 Test Accommodation Form
DISABILITY RESOURCE CENTER
SAN JOSE STATE UNIVERSITY
Administration Building, Rm. 110 • (408)924-6000 • www.drc.sjsu.edu

Testing Hours: Monday-Thursday 9:00AM–8:00PM and Friday 9:00AM–4:00PM
*Students must return forms to the DRC at least **one week** prior to the exam date.•*

Form invalid unless embossed by DRC Seal

The University must comply with federal and state laws, and the California State University policies requiring the prompt delivery of reasonable accommodations to students with disabilities. At SJSU the Disability Resource Center (DRC) is responsible for verifying disability(ies) and presenting appropriate accommodations. If you are unable to accommodate this student as presented below, contact the DRC immediately.

Student: _____ Phone: _____ Student ID#: _____

Professor: _____ Course: _____

*November 11, 2011 • Deadline date to submit forms for FINAL EXAMS

PART I: Prescribed accommodations approved by DRC counselor: _____

Extended time: **2X**
-**Distraction reduced environment**

☐ Alternative Format *If alternative format is required, exam must be submitted 5 days prior to scheduled date.*

- -

Student and Professor must agree on the DATE & TIME
Exam Date: _____ Exam Start Time: _____ Standard time to complete exam: _____

PART II: TO BE COMPLETED BY THE PROFESSOR

Professor INITIALS required for each approved aid. Use of aids will NOT be honored without INITIALS.

☑ **Exam Method of Delivery**   ☑ **Exam Method of Return**
   Check only one   *Check only one*

☐ Email   ☐ Professor pick up
  exams@drc.sjsu.edu
☐ Professor   ☐ Fax: _____
☐ DRC Fax: ☐ Email: _____
  (405)924-6185   *email address*

NO AIDS _____   Book _____
Calculator _____   Notes _____
Other _____

Special instructions to proctor:
_____
_____

For fax or email delivery, please indicate course, exam date, and student's last name either in fax cover or in email body.

Professor's signature: _I have read and agree to date & time of exam_ Office & Cell Phone Numbers: _____
(must be an original signature for each exam)

A copy of this form is available upon request.   Reprinted by permission of the San Jose State University Disability Resource Center.

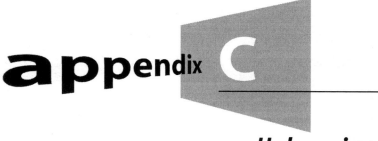

appendix C

Unlearning Exercise

OUR DEFINITION OF UNLEARNING:

Contrary to learning, which is often an unconscious process, unlearning means consciously engaging in an investigation of one's own inner beliefs; unlearning means self-reflection and opening one's mind to diverse viewpoints—consequently offering the possibility for social change.

Step 1: Defining and Evaluating the Process of Unlearning
What do *you* think is the difference between learning and unlearning? Write a list of behaviors and/or attitudes you wish you could unlearn.

Step 2: Assessing the Current Situation
Take a look at the list you just created. Choose one item, and then initiate the unlearning process by assessing the current situation: How did you learn this behavior/attitude? How/why is it important for you to unlearn it? How does it affect you and your relationships with others?

Step 3: Progressing to Initiating Change
Review the notes you created in step 2. Now take a look at the behavior/attitude you noted and write down the things that work and that don't work, preferably in the form of a table. This enables you to analyze the behavior/attitude in further detail by thinking about how it both positively and negatively affects you and your relationships with others.

Step 4: Transforming Learned Behavior
Work off the table to create guidelines and tips you feel would help with moving to the next level, the level that can really initiate change of that specific behavior/attitude. Be creative! Post these guidelines in a place where you can see them all the time. Then, start following those tips and guidelines.

Step 5: Continuing the Transformation Process
Regularly evaluate your transformation process of the desired behavior/attitude change. Have you changed? How useful/not useful were your guidelines in the process? If you have to do any adjustments on the guidelines sheet, do so.

appendix D

Some More Reading

If you are interested in reading more, we found these readings, in addition to those in the reference section, very insightful:

Brightman, Alan. (2008). *DisabilityLand*. New York: SelectBooks, Inc.

Fassett, D.L. (2011). Critical reflections on a pedagogy of ability. In T. Nakayama & R.T. Halualani (Eds.), *The handbook of critical intercultural communication*. New York: Blackwell.

Fassett, D.L., & Morella, D.L. (2008). Remaking (the) discipline: Marking the performative accomplishment of (dis)ability. *Text and Performance Quarterly, 28,* 139-156.

Freire, P. (2003). *Pedagogy of the oppressed: 30th Anniversary Edition*. New York: Continuum.

Galloway, T. (2009). *Mean little deaf queer*. Boston: Beacon Press.

SOME REFERENCES

These references helped us with making sense of some of our experiences and with starting the conversations:

Braithwaite, D.O., & Labrecque, D. (1994). Responding to the Americans with disabilities act: Contributions of interpersonal communication research and training. *Journal of Applied Communication Research, 22*, 287-294.

Cook, G. (2012, November 29). The autism advantage. *The New York Times*. Retrieved from http://www.nytimes.com/2012/12/02/magazine/the-autism-advantage.html?pagewanted=all&_r=0

Disability Resource Center. (2006). Fast facts for faculty. Retrieved May 3, 2013, from San José State University website: http://www.sjsu.edu/drc/faculty/fast-facts/

Disability Resource Center. Syllabus statement rationale. Retrieved May 3, 2013, from San José State University website: http://www.sjsu.edu/drc/faculty/syllabus-statement-rationale/

El-Sharif, Y. (2012). Arbeitsmarkt: Firmen kaufen sich von Behinderten frei. *Spiegel Online*. Retrieved from http://www.spiegel.de/wirtschaft/soziales/schwerbehinderte-verlierer-auf-dem-arbeitsmarkt-a-870630.html

Fassett, D.L., & Warren, J.T. (2007). *Critical communication pedagogy*. Thousand Oaks, CA: Sage.

Freire, P. (2003). *Pedagogy of the oppressed: 30th Anniversary Edition*. New York: Continuum.

Hernandez, B., & McDonald, K. (2007). Exploring the bottom line: A study of the costs and benefits of workers with disabilities. *The Economic Impact Study*. Retrieved May 3, 2013, from http://www.disabilityworks.org/downloads/disabilityworksDePaulStudyComprehensiveResults.pdf

hooks, b. (1994). *Teaching to transgress: Education as the practice of freedom*. New York: Routledge.

Palmer, P.J. (1998). *The courage to teach: Exploring the inner landscape of a teacher's life*. San Francisco: Jossey-Bass.

Pollock, D. (2006). Memory, remembering, and histories of change: A performance praxis. In D.S. Madison & J. Hamera (Eds.), *The Sage handbook of performance studies*, pp. 87-105. Thousand Oaks, CA: Sage.

Spano, S. (2010, Spring). *Training manual & resource guide*. COMM 241R: San José State University.

Stewart, W.F., Ricci, J.A., Chee, E., Hahn, S.R., & Morganstein, D. (2003). Cost of lost productive work time among US workers with depression. *The Journal of the American Medical Association, 289*(23), 3135-3144. doi:10.1001/jama.289.23.3135.

Tapper, J. (2009). Obama apologizes for calling his bad bowling 'Like the special olympics.' *ABC News/Politics*. Retrieved May 3, 2013, from http://abcnews.go.com/Politics/story?id=7129997&page=1

The soldier's creed. (2005). *Army study guide*. Retrieved May 3, 2013, from http://www.armystudyguide.com/content/Prep_For_Basic_Training/Prep_for_basic_general_information/the-soldiers-creed.shtml

United Nations. Convention on the Rights of Persons with Disabilities. (2006). Some facts about persons with disabilities. Retrieved May 5, 2013, from http://www.un.org/disabilities/convention/facts.shtml

U.S. Census Bureau. (2008). Americans with disabilities: 2005. Retrieved May 5, 2013, from http://www.census.gov/prod/2008pubs/p70-117.pdf

U.S. Department of Justice, Civil Rights Division, Disability Rights Section, Americans with Disabilities Act. (2009). *A guide to disability rights laws*. Retrieved May 2, 2013, from http://www.ada.gov/cguide.htm#anchor62335

U.S. Department of Labor, Bureau of Labor Statistics. (2012). *Persons with a disability: Labor force characteristics summary* (BLS Economic Releases No. USDL-12-1125). Retrieved May 2, 2013, from http://www.bls.gov/news.release/disabl.nr0.htm

Zeff, R. (2007). Universal design across the curriculum. *New Directions for Higher Education, 137*, 27-44.